Goddess
of the
Ancient Maya

Goddess

of the
Ancient Maya

"The hidden primal Goddess of Creation
in Maya mythology"

Douglas T. Peck

COPYRIGHT © 2008 BY DOUGLAS T. PECK.

LIBRARY OF CONGRESS CONTROL NUMBER:		2008906589
ISBN:	HARDCOVER	978-1-4363-5866-8
	SOFTCOVER	978-1-4363-5865-1

This book was printed in the United States of America.

Other books by Douglas T. Peck:

Cristoforo Colombo: God's Navigator: ISBN 0-9641798-0-6, copyright 1993, Columbian Publishers, Columbus, WI.

Ponce de Leon and the Discovery of Florida. ISBN: 1-880654-02-4, copyright 1993, Pogo Press, St. Paul, MN.

The Yucatan: From Prehistoric Times to the Great Maya Revolt of 1546. ISBN 1-4134-8926-5, copyright 2005, Xlibris Corporation, Philadelphia.

Origin and Diffusion of Maya Civilisation. ISBN: 978-1-4257-2449-8, copyright 2007, Xlibris Corporation, Philadelphia.

Other historical literary works by Douglas T. Peck, see: www.NewWorldExplorersInc.org

To order additional copies of this book, contact:
Xlibris Corporation
1-888-795-4274
www.Xlibris.com
Orders@Xlibris.com
51830

Contents

Dedication

Dedicated to Enriqita M. de Avila

The "Goddess" of Isla Mujeres

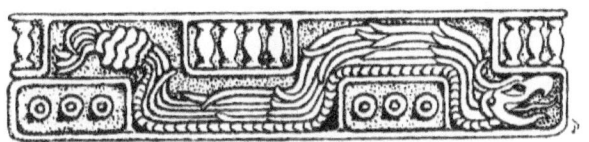

List of Illustrations

(Except where noted all illustrations are original art by the author)

Acknowledgements

Even though it may seem unlikely, my historical research on the voyages of early Spanish explorers to the shores of Mexico was tied into and a vital part of this work on the history of Olmec/Maya religion. So my acknowledgements must start with my entry into the discipline of historical research in 1986 when I became associated with the Society for the History of Discoveries (SHD). My colleagues in the SHD, probably without realizing it, played an important role in preparation and writing of this book. Their expertise in the discipline of historical research was unselfishly shared with me in my sometimes agonizing transition from an ocean navigator and geographer to research historian. Included in this group of astute scholars are John Parker, Carol Urness, Ursula Lamb, James E. Kelley Jr., Oliver Dunn, David Henige, Helen Wallace, Donald McGuirk, Gregory McIntosh, Charles Hoffman, and Dan Amato. I distributed drafts of my work to these scholars and they kindly took the time to critique the papers and offer suggestions related to the accuracy and readability of the content.

My earlier research and writing had been largely centered on the seafaring and navigation expertise of the first Spanish explorers of the New World. But in my research of the voyage of Francisco Hernández de Córdoba's 1517 discovery of Yucatan and his encounter with the Maya my interests changed direction to a study of the origin and development of this enigmatic advanced culture and polity. When I expanded my studies to include the prehistoric Maya in Yucatan I moved from the assistance of most of my SHD colleagues and was introduced to a new but equally helpful and cooperative group of Mexican scholars. My full-time library and field research in the history of the ancient Maya occupied well over a decade and included forty-two weeks visiting university and museum archives in Merida, Cancun, Guadalajara, and Chetumal, as well as the major archaeological sites in Yucatan.

In my extensive research in Yucatan I was blessed with having the acquaintance of several good friends who are bilingual in English and Spanish and graciously gave me immeasurable assistance in my travels and contacts during my research efforts. Gerardo Magaña Barragan is the Director of the Regional Turismo Office on Isla Mujeres, former Mayor (Presidente) of Isla Mujeres, and former teacher in the Cancun/Isla Mujeres school system. Gerardo not only introduced me to key educators and civic leaders in the area, but translated several of my papers on the Maya into Spanish for distribution within the regional school system. Early in my historical research (1996) Gerardo introduced me to Dr. Ricardo Delphin Quezada Dominguez, Faculty Director of Universidad Autonoma de Yucatan in Merida. Dr. Quezada kindly arranged for me to present a formal lecture to the advanced students after which in a meeting with key faculty members we engaged in a lively discussion of early Maya history. During my two day stay at the University Dr. Quezada presented me with a considerable number of copies of historical documents on early Maya history that are only available to faculty members.

To add to the store of valuable reference material I received from Universidad and Museum archives, Senior Jesus Lima, the Grand Old Man of Isla Mujeres and a legend in his time, gave me several scarce documents on early sixteenth-century Spanish/Maya encounters from his extensive private library. From these documents, many predating Spanish conquest, I learned the true story of the legendary and ethereal Maya hero, Jacinta Canek, which is far removed from the inaccurate accounts in current historiography. In this extended field research I depended on both Gerardo Magaña and Enriquita M. de Avila to act as my translators. Enriquita was a well-known and talented artist of the area and willingly and quite effectively acted as my translator and coordinator in my travels around the area. She is better organized than I am and she faithfully kept track of and reminded me of my appointments and schedule. In her tireless dedication to helping others, Enriquita was overtaken by chronic heart failure and it is with respect that this book is dedicated to her memory.

In 1997 and again in 2001, Dr. Mariano Ceballos Martinez, Director Academico of La Salle Universidad in Cancun kindly invited me to present papers to the advanced students. At La Salle Universidad, in like manner to my experience in the Universidad in Merida, these visits were followed by a lengthy discussion of early Maya history with faculty archaeologists and historians Juan E. Vanegas Perez, Luis Armando Guillermo, and Rubin Cruz Carena. These discussions only lightly touched on the subject of Maya religion, but I did learn that these Mexican scholars considered the *Popol Vuh* as relatively unimportant folklore with little appearance of true history.

Preface

This book related to an early concept of religion is unique in that it was written by a pragmatic historian rather an anthropologist, archeologist, theologian, or philosophical humanist. But following proven guidelines for historical research I have drawn from the writings of all these related disciplines to arrive at a pattern for the development of the Maya pantheon of gods beginning with the little-known and unreported ancient Goddess of Creation through the Formative and Classic period to Spanish conquest in the sixteenth-century. The primary theme of this book follows the evolution of the ancient Goddess of Creation concept into the firmly embedded and widely accepted concept of a male Creator or God of Creation that has been spearheaded by Judeo/Christian and Islamic religious dogma. From early times, dating back to the Second-Century Roman period of Constantine the Great, the omnipotent power of these two dominant religions has suppressed (at times in a brutal and violent fashion) any attempt to present a contrary view or concept of Creation.

This barrier to freethinking and astute historical research was breached by the relatively recent writings of Rachel Levy, *The Gate of Horn: A Study of the Religious Conceptions of the Stone Age and Their Influence upon European Thought* (1948), Raphael Patai, *The Hebrew Goddess* (1967), and Merlin Stone, *When God Was a Woman* (1976). The writings of Levy, Patai and Stone opened the door for a number of scholarly works on the subject, the most prominent being those by Monica Sjoo and Barbara Mor (1987), Elenor Gadon (1989), Marija Gimbutes (1999), and Barbara Tedlock (2005). These published works related to the early primal goddesses are almost exclusively confined to the religious concepts of Europe and the Middle-East.

Tatiana Proskouriakoff, Rosemary Joyce, and Traci Ardren have written extensively relative to the role of the female in Maya history, but these works, related to the political and social role of Maya women, are confined to the Classic and Post-Classic period and do not address the primal Maya Goddess of Creation concept which is the primary thrust of this book (Ardren 2002; Joyce 1992, 1993, 2000; Proskouriakoff 1961, 1963, 1964). And the available published works of archaeologists that provide brief coverage of early religious concepts of the Olmec/Maya, particularly those related to primal gods and goddesses, are incomplete, inaccurate and of little value. The inadequate research and presentation of this important subject of the role that primal Olmec/Maya goddesses played in development of their later religious concepts is corrected by this book.

The Maya Kukulcan/Itzamna religious mythology in which the goddess Ix Chel is shown as directly descended from the primal "First Mother" is one of the great ancient religious myths of Creation contemporary with the well known Eastern European and Middle-Eastern Zoroastrian, Phrygian, Sumerian, Mycenaean, and Judaic-Christian-Islamic mythological mystique of Creation. But current anthropologist/historians have failed to recognize that fact because of the almost naïve belief that the convoluted and contrived colonial period folklore from questionable sources (primarily the Aztec *Legenda de los Soles* and the Quiche *Popol Vuh* (described without viable reason as the "Bible" of the Maya) constituted an accurate view of Maya history related to their cultural and religious development. These late works of patently contrived folklore from unknown sources picture Maya religious concepts as crude, primitive, often grotesque fables rather than the true, sophisticated and realistic religious concepts expressed in their writings and art.

Part I presents a study of the origins of the Olmec/Proto-Maya religion from archaic times to the late Formative period where it had evolved into the Kukulcan/Itzamna religious concept. An inherent part of this study is a review of ancient world-wide concepts of a primordial Mother Goddess or Goddess of Creation that are related to the Creation mystique of the Maya. However, any suggestion that the culture of indigenous peoples of Mesoamerica has been influenced or has any relevancy to those of other cultures is zealously rejected by archaeologists who have adopted without reservation the poorly supported, even manifestly unfounded, "Indigenous (Internalist, Social Evolution) Theory" that Mesoamerican cultures developed entirely within the American continent without any inter-hemispheric influence.

Part II contains the primary thesis of the book in following development of the Maya pantheon of gods from its late Formative period origin through the Classic period and into the early period of Spanish conquest. Maya religion is shown to have developed a historical pattern common to world-wide religions discussed earlier in which the primal Goddess of Creation concept has been gradually changed or evolved into a patriarchal form of a male supreme god with the original primal goddess relegated to a lesser role among other gods. This study shows in Part I how the socially powerful Judeo/Christian and Islamic religions were responsible for suppressing the ancient Goddess religions in Europe and the Middle-East. And in Part II this same scenario is shown to have been repeated in the Americas where the suppression of the ancient Olmec/Proto-Maya Goddess of Creation concept has come full-circle in the *Popol Vuh* with the primal goddess Ix Chel mentioned (by another name) only briefly on the first page and thereafter lost from view by the prominent roles given to the male "Hero Twins" and the supreme Christianized male God known as "Heart of Sky" or Heaven. Because of the controversial nature of the subject; both evidence and argument is presented to support each conclusion as well as a critical review of opposing views. In this respect the book is both a history of the subject and a study of the historiography of the subject.

The Epilogue is an important part of the book in giving a brief overview of the colonial period transition or integration of Maya religious concepts into their adopted Christian Faith.

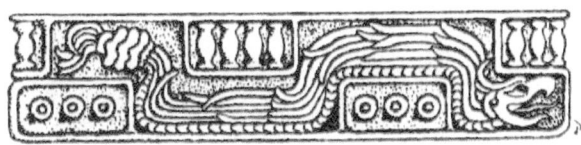

Part I

The Hidden "Goddess of Creation" in Olmec/Proto-Maya Mythology

The Olmec and later Maya primal gods were dominated by male figures, but a searching examination of art and sculpture related to their religious mythology and pantheon of gods reveals evidence of an almost hidden and unreported primary role of the female in their mystical creation of the earth and cosmos and in later symbolic creation of mortal god-kings. In primitive societies world-wide the primal female goddess of creation dating back to the Paleolithic period preceded the later male gods and this study presents viable evidence that this was the case in the unrecorded, unclear, and controversial early mythology of the Olmec/Proto-Maya.

The ontological study of prehistoric Olmec/Proto-Maya religion is difficult for the historian and archaeologist because it demands knowledge of abstract thinking and views that can only be explicitly expressed orally or in contemporary prehistoric written documents, neither of which are available for study of the subject. Instead, the religious mystique and dogma of these ancient peoples must be deduced by analogical reasoning from examination of their pictorial art and sculptures, a task that is not necessarily limited to the scientific approach of the archaeologists on the scene. Roberta and Peter Markman in their study of Mesoamerican religions (Markman-Markman 1989) noted that the ubiquitous sculptured masks found throughout the region provided a metaphorical representation of the nature and source of a particular god. And I have used this same historical research approach except that I have broadened my study beyond masks to view all art and sculpture of the Olmec/Proto-Maya as a metaphor for a particular god or concept of religious mystique.

The worldwide origin and early acceptance of the primal Mother Goddess or Goddess of Creation

Answering a driving force inherent in the genes and psyche of all mankind, no matter how scattered among the continents and islands of the world, the earliest religious concepts were centered on the Earth Mother and the mystery of reproduction and creation of life. In the late Paleolithic period (35,000-10,000 BC) there is ample evidence that the mystery of human female birth or creation dominated religious oriented art in Europe, the Middle-East, Africa and ostensibly many other areas throughout the inhabited world although these are the primary sites that have been investigated. The first known human images are the numerous small and widely distributed so-called "Venus" figurines carved from stone, bone, ivory, or fashioned from clay. These figurines (Figure 1) have exaggerated female body features associated with pregnancy and childbirth. There is no attempt to include facial features so they were not intended to represent or be portraits of a particular mortal person. Instead the lower part of the legs and feet are fashioned with a shapeless point intended to be thrust into the ground, held by hand, or fastened on the end of a staff to be used as a religious icon in some undetermined religious ritual. These icons; found in cave hearths, alter niches, and graves, quite apparently represented the first depiction of the female Goddess of Creation.

In the late Paleolithic period, contemporary with development of the Goddess of Creation in human form, the earth was considered a female spirit with magical power of giving or creating life. The deceased were buried in a fetal position with the bones painted red to prepare them for rebirth from Mother Earth. In addition to the Venus figurines there are numerous cave drawings indicating that human birth was considered a mystical spiritual event (Figure 2) rather than just a mundane biological bodily function. Barbara Mor in concert with Mircea Eliade indicated: "The Earth was seen by all primal people as the source of nourishment, protection, power, and the mystery of cyclic recurrence. Perhaps the first human analogy made was between the earth and a female, who performed the same functions on an individual level. Especially awesome was the woman's ability to bleed rhythmically with the moon's phases, and her periodic swelling up and dramatic expulsion [creation] of a new being.

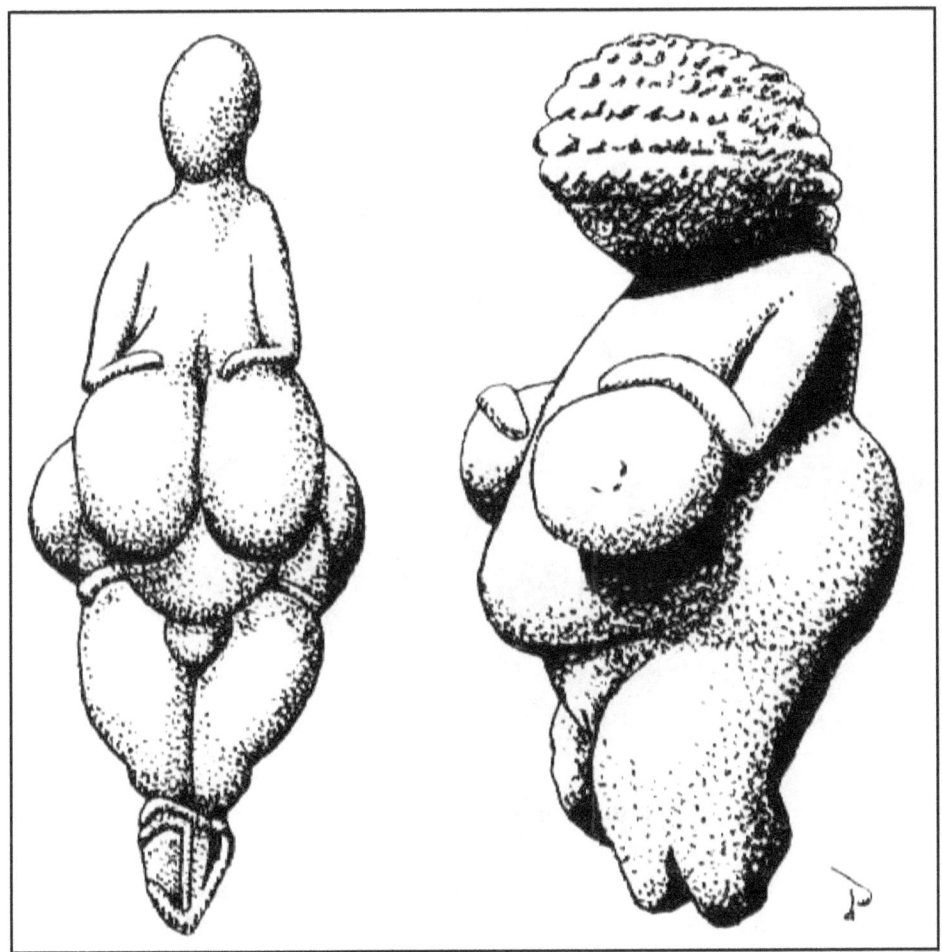

Figure 1: Drawings of the Venus of Lespugue (left) and Venus of Willendorf (right).

To imagine the enormous impact of pregnancy and childbirth on our human ancestors, we have to remember that Paleolithic people, like many primitive aboriginal people today, did not know the connection between intercourse and pregnancy; and the pregnancy itself was seen as resulting from a magical intercourse between the mother and the spirit world—or it was seen as a parthenogenetic act, the woman as spontaneous and autonomous creator of life" (Sjoo-Mor (1987:47; Eliade 1964).

In Europe and the Middle-East the Mother-Earth Goddess and the human appearing Goddess of Creation evolved from Paleolithic times to Biblical times into more sophisticated and complex forms. The most prominent documented primal goddesses of ancient societies were Inanna

3

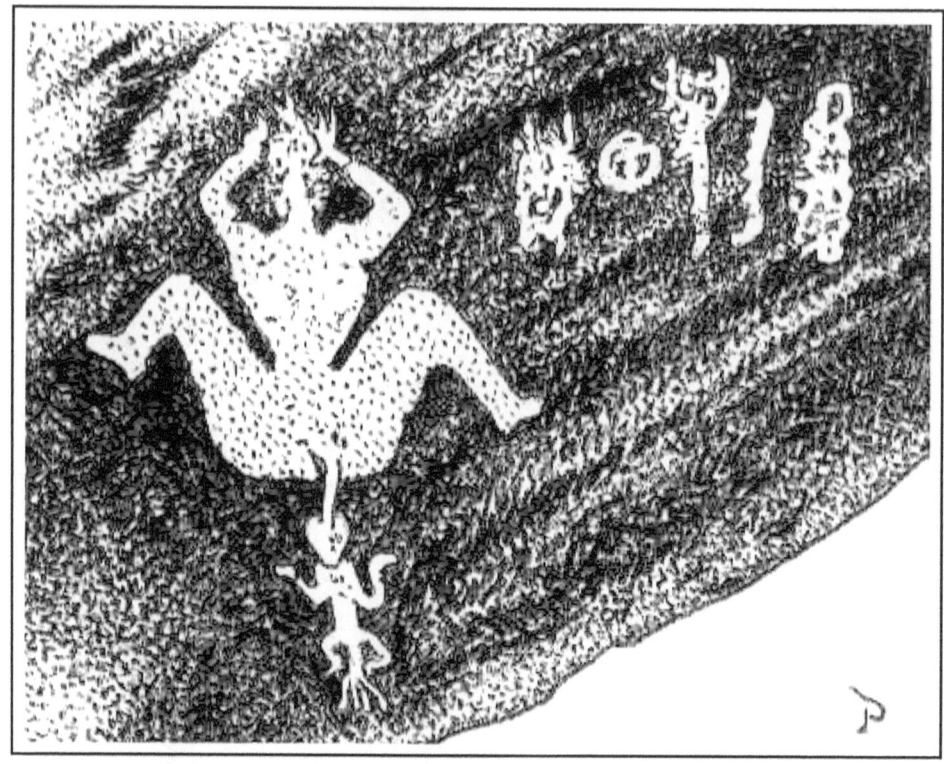

Figure 2: Paleolithic rock drawing of a woman giving birth found in a cave in Yemen. The female figure appears to be wearing a mask and the line inscriptions to the right of the figure are suggestive of early logographic writing which would relate the birth to a mystical event of Creation rather than a common normal birth. After Sjoo-Mor (1987).

the Sumerian Mother-Goddess, Artemas the Mycenaean and Greek "Life Giver" goddess (Gadon 1989:115-187; Gimbutas 1999:155-157), and Asherah (Astarte) in ancient pre-biblical Israel, with Asherah mentioned more than forty times in the Bible as the abominable "Queen of Heaven" (Patai 1978). The history of the long and troubled struggle of Semitic priests to replace pagan goddess religions with a monotheistic and patriarchal religion is reported in detail in the Judaic-Christian Old Testament (Laymon 1971:1-133, 320-324, 329-404, 579-580) and to a lesser and unclear extent the Islamic Qur'an (Yusuf Ali 2001:24-26, 340-389, 439-440, 1519-1549). The final triumph of this struggle banning pagan goddess religions came about from two epic historical events; (1) when Emperor Constantine in about AD 300 made Christianity the official religion of the wide realm of Rome and

(2) throughout the Middle-East with the rise to power of Mohammed in the seventh-century which established strict adherence to the extreme patriarchal Islamic religion expressed in the Qur'an (Yusaf Ali 2001). This same general scenario of a patriarchal religion replacing an earlier primal matriarchal goddess religion, but in a modified form, can be seen in the development of the Olmec/Proto-Maya religion and their pantheon of gods.

The Olmec/Proto-Maya Mountain of Creation

There is nearly universal agreement that the earliest Olmec in the Gulf coastal area would have revered the huge and active volcano named San Martin Pajapán in the nearby Tuxtla mountains as the sacred Mountain of Creation and abode of their gods. Referring to the volcano San Martin Pajapán, Linda Schele concluded that; "volcanoes and cleft-mountains were a prominent feature in Olmec art and representing openings between this world and the Otherworld. For the Olmec's, the ordering of the earth and sky apparently took place atop the great volcano that was the source of creative force within their world." (Freidel-Schele-Parker 1993:132-133). A sculptured life-size statue of an Olmec god-king wearing the headdress of a cleft-headed god and a maize plant was found in what constituted a cleft between the two highest peaks of San Martin Pajapán crater (Figure 3) lending further evidence that the volcano was the Olmec Mountain of Creation and abode of their gods. The V-shaped cleft or inverted triangle has been used since Paleolithic times as a symbol for the female vagina, representing the origin of life and creation (Gadon 1989:3-85; Leeming 2005:155-158; Markman-Markman 1989:14-15). It then follows that the San Martin Pajapán volcano was considered by the Olmec as a primal female Mountain Goddess of Creation

In mythology of ancient cultures from around the world, mountains have served as the sacred home of their gods in a similar fashion to Olmec tradition. In Greece, Mount Olympus was the home of the Olympian gods. In ancient Sumer and Babylon, the temples known as ziggurats (the equivalent of the Olmec/Maya pyramidal temple) represented their "Holy Mountain" and home of the Mother Goddess Inanna. Canaanite gods such as El and Baal were divinities of their "Holy Mountain." The Phrygian "Mother Goddess" Cyble was the Mountain Goddess from whom Moses received godly instructions, and in ancient China mountains were seen as living earth-divinities that had the power to send the essential rain (Leeming 2005:4,63,68,75,90,187,259,271; Gadon 1989:115-187).

Figure 3: Drawing of a life-size stature of an Olmec king wearing a headdress of a cleft-headed god or goddess found in a cleft of the San Martin Pajapán volcano in the Tuxtla Mountains.

The prominent role of mountains in later religious mythology derived from Olmec tradition is also revealed in the creation mystique of the Mixtec

Figure 4:   Drawing of *Yax-Hai-Witz*, the Maya Mountain of Creation in carved
            sculpture on the Palenque Tablet of the Foliated Cross. After Freidel-
            Schele-Parker (1993).

in east-central Mexico. In the Mixtec myth the First Father was known
as Jaguar Lion and the First Mother was a very beautiful princess who
was known as Jaguar Serpent. When these two primal gods appeared in
a dark chaotic world of water, slime, and mud, they made a huge rock or
mountain for their dwelling on earth and at the highest point of their house
they placed a copper axe with the blade turned upward to the sky (Leon-
Portillo,-Shorris 2001:619-620). There are two elements of this Mixtec
myth of creation that are reminiscent of Olmec mythology of creation; the
first is the name of the primal gods with names related to Jaguar/Serpent,
and the other is the upturned axe at the top of the mountain reminiscent
of the mystique incumbent in the Olmec clefted Mountain of Creation and
later cleft-headed gods many of which show a pointed axe-like protrusion
issuing from the cleft instead of a maize plant.

The mystique of the Olmec Mountain of Creation was carried into
Maya religious mythology in the late Formative period and was known as
Yax-Hai-Witz. The mountain of *Yax-Hai-Witz* was shown on the Palenque
Tablet of the Foliated Cross (Figure 4) and identified as a large Earth or
Mountain God with a cleft head from which sprouted numerous maize

Figure 5: Drawing of a low-relief sculpture found on a hillside near Chalcatzingo showing an Olmec god-king in a religious mountain cave ritual. After Luckert (1976).

plants. Linda Schele has shown that this Maya Mountain of Creation was one of several other related religious icons and symbols inherited from the Olmec indicating that the Maya basic religious concept of Creation was inherited, or more correctly brought by the Olmec to the Maya in the Formative or Preclassic period (Freidel-Schele-Parker 1993:138-139). The Olmec/Maya Mountain God *Yax-Hai-Witz* as shown in Figure 4 can be related to the Olmec by the cleft-head sprouting maize plants and the large goggle-eyes, prominent features found in numerous early gods of the Olmec. There is clear evidence that the primal Olmec Mountain of Creation (see Figure 5) was a Mother-Goddess in the Formative period, but with the change to a patriarchal religion in an unclear later period; the *Yax-Hai-Witz* pictured in Palenque may have evolved into a Maya male god.

The several stylized cave openings in the depiction of *Yax-Hai-Witz* the Maya Mountain God can also be related to the numerous stylized depictions of caves in the Olmec Mountain of Creation which served for the ritual re-enactment of the creation myth by Olmec god-kings. One of the several carvings related to caves in the Olmec Mountain of Creation (Duran 1971:237-238; Grove 1984:21) was found on a hill overlooking Chalcatzingo, a major Olmec site locating west of Tres Zapotes. The Chalcatzingo carving shows a Creation ritual performed by an Olmec god-king seated in a cave opening that is a highly stylized mouth of a serpent. Since the serpent is frequently represented as a symbol for Mother Earth, Markman has interpreted the cave opening in the ritual as a metaphor for the vagina of the primal Earth Mother or Goddess, and thus suggests the primal creation mythology of the Olmec included an Earth Mother or Goddess prior to the appearance of the male were-jaguar figures (Markman-Markman 1989:14-16) The eye of the serpent contains the fire of a volcano eruption which could tie the depicted ritual to the revered Olmec Mountain of Creation, the San Martin Pajapán active volcano in the Tuxtla mountain range. The god-king in the ritual holds a large stylized depiction of the earth in his lap that is reminiscent of the earth monster or serpent held by the later Olmec primal God of Creation in Figure 3. The sexual connotation of the ritual involving birth or creation is clearly indicated by the clouds overhead raining phallic shaped raindrops onto Mother Earth to produce a bountiful harvest of maize plants pictured throughout the scene.

The Olmec were-jaguar god: A male, female, or unisex god?

At an unclear time during the Formative period the Olmec primal Goddess of Creation was replaced as the principal god of the Olmec by a supernatural composite figure labeled a were-jaguar. Matthew Stirling (1965:716-738; 1967:1-8) and Miguel Covarrubias (1946:97-

99; 1957:56-83) set the stage for the popular and accepted view that the primal god of the Olmec was a male were-jaguar ("were" is Old English for man or human) combining the features and presumably the traits of both a human and a jaguar (Benson 1998:53-76; Coe 1972:1-12, 1993:38-40, 2002:75-76; Saunders 1998:12-52) Covarrubias passes over the incongruity of an advanced agricultural society having as their major god one that was related to a hunter/jaguar oriented society in stating: "I have insisted that the jaguar dominated the art of La Venta. This jaguar fixation [of Covarrubias, but not necessarily of the Olmec] must have had a religious motivation, either totemic or related to the cult of the early rain and earth spirits conceived as jaguars" (Covarrubias 1957:58). To state that the Olmec "conceived the early rain and earth spirits as jaguars" is patently unsupported conjecture and Covarrubias throws a shadow on that conclusion by noting that many of the early Mesoamerican societies had primary deities associated with the serpent rather than the jaguar which he speculated were derived from an unclear and poorly verified mythical "sky dragon" (Covarrubias 1957:60-63). Not only "many of the early Mesoamerican societies" had a serpent as their principal god but recent published research has established that the Olmec were the originators of the feathered serpent god adopted by the Maya as Kukulcan and much later in a perverted form adopted in the highlands as Quetzalcoatl (Peck 2002:10-12; Peck 2005:32-34, 71-73).

To support the Jaguar origin of the were-jaguar god Matthew Stirling asserted that an Olmec sculpture he had found in Portrero Nuevo realistically portrayed a jaguar in the act of copulation with a human female (Stirling 1955:19). Michael Coe provided strong support for Stirling's conclusion related to the were-jaguar god when he identified the numerous plump baby figurines found throughout the Olmec area as, "were-jaguar babies, offspring of feline father and human mother, deities of thunder, lightening and rain" (Coe 1965a). It is unclear, even manifestly illogical, why plump babies should be "deities of thunder, lightening, and rain." In another treatise on the subject of Jaguar-human copulation to explain the were-jaguar figures Coe concluded; "that this union resulted in a race of infants combining the features of a jaguar and man in varying degrees. These are usually shown as somewhat infantile throughout life, with the puffy features of small fat babies, snarling mouths, fangs, and perhaps even claws. They are always quite sexless, with the obesity of eunuchs" (Coe 1965b:751-752). There are a few figurines that could be interpreted as babies with "puffy features" and the exaggerated facial

Figure 6: A cave drawing in Guerrero showing copulation between a male human and a female jaguar. After Guthrie (1995).

features of a were-jaguar but the large majority of these recorded figurines (Guthrie 1995:130-134, 235) are just what they represented; natural life-like "small fat babies" with no indication of a relationship to the fierce, supernatural, and cleft-headed were-jaguar gods.

Close examination of the Olmec works of art that are used to support the copulation hypothesis only show humans being attacked by jaguars without even a hint at sexual activity. The only definitively explicit drawing of copulation between a human and a jaguar (Figure 6) found in a cave in Guerrero (Diehl-Coe 1995:20, Fig. 16) is of questionable Olmec origin. This drawing shows copulation between a male human and a female jaguar rather than vice-versa as in Stirling's and Coe's interpretation of Olmec art. This undated drawing is not in Olmec art style and probably relates to contrived late folklore of a daring macho-male regional and legendary hero who claimed to have raped jaguars rather than a more realistic view of early Olmec religious mythology.

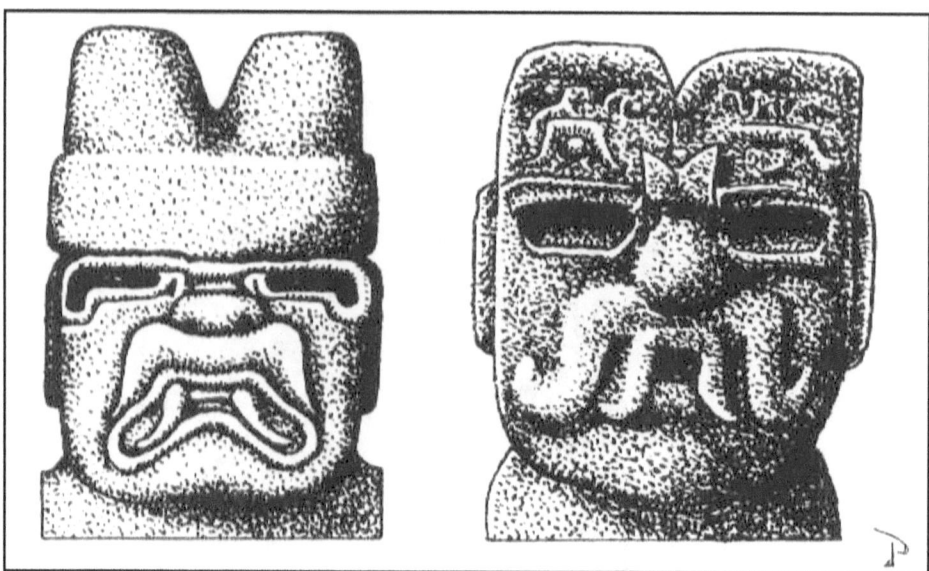

Figure 7: Two typical Olmec anthropomorphous were-jaguar figures with cleft-heads. After Guthrie (1995).

Historians in their fixation with jaguars have not considered that the unclear and questionable jaguar features in Olmec figures soon gave way to serpent features and the ubiquitous cleft-head, a symbol for the female vagina representing the origin of life and creation, which has little or no relation to a jaguar, is by far the most significant (and numerically most abundant) feature to identify the role and importance of the pictured god in the Olmec pantheon of gods. Although the supernatural animal-like features of the were-jaguar cannot be identified as male or female the human Olmec style flowing moustache common to many of the figures is male related and this together with the female cleft-head symbol would indicate that these anthropomorphous figures were intended to be parthenogenesis or unisex gods. But this realistic view of this prominent Olmec god is far from that contained in current historiography.

Historians that have noted the cleft-head as a female symbol for procreation have failed to associate it in a definitive manner with the Primal God of Creation and instead have postulated a variety of Olmec gods with unclear roles in Olmec religion. Michael Coe postulated six different Olmec gods (Coe 1968:41-78) and David Joralemon proposed ten gods (Joralemon 1971) primarily patterned after Aztec gods with animal features combined into supernatural humanoid composite forms and considered the cleft-head of little definitive diagnostic value since it is only

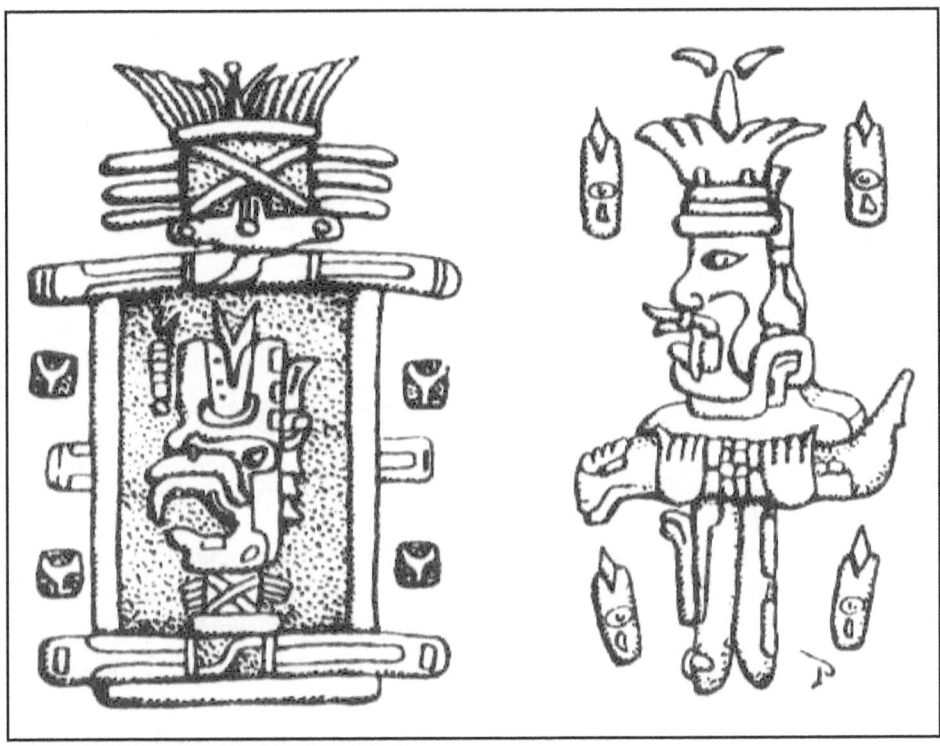

Figure 8: Two depictions of the Olmec unisex God of Creation showing the cleft-head and creation of both maize plants and the four corners of the earth and cosmos. After Guthrie (1995).

presented in random fashion on several of their postulated gods. Beatriz de la Fuente among others faulted Joralemon's and Coe's questionable identification of Olmec gods because the conclusions were "based on a comparison of the Aztec with the Olmec, the cultures having between them a span of some 2000 to 2500 years" (De la Fuente 1991:89).

Rather than the numerous contrived Olmec gods proposed by many prominent historians the Olmec God of Creation that appeared on the scene after the earlier primal Mother Goddess of Creation was the unisex god pictured in early Olmec art creating the four corners of the earth and sky and the life sustaining maize plant. Figure 8 contains two examples of this later God of Creation which has the appearance of a male, but the prominent female cleft of the goddess in the head of the god and in the maize kernels at the four corners of the earth would fix this as a parthenogenesis or unisex god. In the evolution of Olmec religious concepts into that of the

13

Figure 9: The drawing on the left showing a bearded Olmec figure emerging from a cleft in the Mountain of Creation (from Taube 1992) was found in a temple in Chichén Itzá. The drawing on the right from Yaxchilan shows a cleft-headed god resembling an Olmec were-jaguar. From Tate (1992).

later Chontal Maya/Itzá religion the cleft head is less pronounced but still found in Classic period art and sculpture. The drawings in Figure 9 show a depiction of the Olmec Mountain of Creation with a cleft-head found in Chichén Itzá and a highly stylized cleft headed Olmec were-jaguar found in Yaxchilan.

With the move of the center of Olmec/Proto-Maya culture and religion to Yucatan (i.e. the Olmec/Chontal/Itzá-Centric Theory) this simple monotheistic unisex god evolved into a more sophisticated patriarchal concept of a supreme First-Father with numerous lesser gods, but the role of the goddess as creator of life was still maintained as an important, even fundamental element of the later Maya religion.

Part II

The Evolution of the Maya Pantheon of Gods from the Formative Period to Spanish Conquest

Common to ancient societies from around the world the Olmec/Maya religious concepts evolved from an initial primal goddess to a later patriarchal supreme god. In Part I the evolution of the primal Mountain Goddess of Creation was traced to the anthropomorphous god improperly labeled a were-jaguar. It was also shown that the so-called were-jaguar figures contained supernatural features that were not limited to a jaguar and the most prominent feature of the symbolic female cleft indicated this evolved god was not a male god as popularly believed, but was conceived as a parthenogenesis or unisex god. And this unisex Olmec god was also associated with creating the life-giving maize and dividing the earth and cosmos into the four cardinal points (Figure 8) a concept amply shown in later Maya religious mythology of creation.

In the Olmec/Chontal/Itzá migration and military conquest of Yucatan in the late Formative period (Peck 2002:9-28; 2005:29-44; 2007:64-90) the Maya concept evolved from the earlier Olmec/Proto-Maya unisex form into the patriarchal male supreme god or "First Father" and a lesser "First Mother" goddess. The Maya mythology of creation contains a glimmering suggestion that the "First Mother" was the initial dominant or supreme goddess rather than the First Father. The Maya account of creation in the Palenque Tablet of the Cross reported the First Mother appeared six years before creation of the earth and sky on Ahaw 18 Tźek—7 December, 3121 BC and 540 days earlier than the First Father on Ahaw 8 Muwan—16 June, 3122 BC (Freidel-Schele-Parker 1995:69). The Tablet of the Cross has not

Figure 10: The public ritualized birth ceremony for Maya kings performed on pyramidal temples revealed by graffiti drawings found in Tikal. After Freidel-Schele-Parker (1993).

been fully deciphered and it is unclear when the First Father became the dominant supreme god of creation. Michael Coe has identified the First Father as Itzamna, the supreme god of the Maya and the First Mother as Ix Chel, who in spite of her earlier manifestation is relegated in later mythology to a lesser role as goddess of fertility and mother of the other Maya gods including the Bacabs (Coe 1993:177).

The association of natural female birth with supernatural creation dating back to Paleolithic times (Figure 2) was reflected in Olmec religious rituals performed on sacred mountains as pictured in the Chalcatzingo carving (Figure 5). This religious ritual not only showed the creation of the earth and ruling gods, but served as the pattern for a ritual to legitimize the Rulership of Maya kings as being descended from a primal god. This Particular Olmec religious tradition associated with Yax-Hai-Witz, the Maya Mountain of Creation would have been carried into Maya religious dogma with the migration and diffusion of Olmec culture into Yucatan in the late Formative period. While the Olmec ritual of supernatural birth or creation was performed on their Mountain of Creation (Figure 5), a related ritual was later performed by the Maya (Figure 10) using a pyramidal temple or replica to represent Yax-Hai-Witz, the Mountain of Creation.

The three crude but pictorially definitive graffiti drawings shown in Figure 10 depict this religious ritual being performed at the top of a

Figure 11: Vase drawing of Maya birthing ritual for Maya kings. After Tedlock (2005)

pyramidal temple (or a stage replica of the temple) representing the sacred Mountain of Creation from Olmec/Proto-Maya mythology establishing it as a religious supernatural creation rather than just a mundane natural birth. The queens are shown in ceremonial garb (two with face masks probably representing Ix Chel, the Maya "First Mother") and with swollen bellies of late pregnancy. The fact that they are late term pregnant females can hardly be doubted since the central figure has the simplistic but recognizable female body form and the figure on the left pictures a rather explicit female vagina. The small seated figures, fully developed and wearing the regalia of kings, have nevertheless just been born, or more properly, created, in this highly orchestrated ritual. I would suggest that the orchestration of this ritual may well have been performed shortly after actual birth elsewhere or included rapidly removing the newborn baby during the public ritual to be replaced by a small, fully dressed, replica of the king seated on his throne, and that was the scene drawn by the artist. Showing ancient god-kings and mythological gods being fully developed and dressed at the moment of birth is common to prehistoric art work. And regarding the public manner of this birth ritual, even into the middle ages the entire Royal Court in most European countries were required to be present at the birth of a king to insure legitimacy of the dynastic lineage.

The three queens are shown wearing different regalia so if it were possible to date the graffiti, the three birth rituals were probably widely separated in time and represent establishment of separate dynasties. Each standing queen is shown grasping a vertical post with a strap from that post passing just under her arms and around her shoulders, while her upper thigh and belly appear to be lashed to some form of support behind her. The queen thus supported could provide the exertion or push for delivery, and aided by gravity, this procedure would probably be an easier and more effective clinical method of delivery than the modern method of lying prone and unsupported. And the figure on the right shows a vague figure in the background that can be construed as a midwife or queen's attendant. These graffiti drawings are not the only depiction of this public ritualized birthing ceremony. A variation of this birthing ritual for Maya queens was shown on a sixth-century vase (Figure 11) in which the standing Queen-Mother was shown grasping two overhead ropes and a midwife reaches from behind and with joined hands supported and provided pressure to the queen's extended belly instead of the lashing shown in the Tikal drawings (Tedlock 2005:215).

This carefully choreographed official state religious ritual constituted much more than just a celebration of the birth of a king. The ritual was symbolically performed on a pyramidal temple representing Yax-Hai-Witz, the Maya Mountain of creation to signify that the newly born king is the rightful mortal heir to the throne as well as a supernatural god-king descended from primal Maya gods. These important and historically significant drawings of a Maya queen-mother's birthing ritual which established the Rulership of the king as both the mortal head-of-state and as a god-king descended from ancient Maya gods have been grossly misinterpreted by prominent archaeologists as simply Maya kings riding in litters. The small lower figures in the right-hand drawing have been labeled by archaeologists as litter bearers, but are more likely spectators. The figure on the extreme right is possibly the one who drew the graffiti and rather than grasping the carrying pole of a litter seems to be finishing his rather crude drawing of a pyramidal temple in the lower right-hand portion, the logical place to finish a drawing.

In an inexplicable failure to grasp the historical significance of these easily recognizable ritual birth ceremonies, leading archaeologists have labeled the drawings as depicting Maya kings riding in litters with their protector gods standing behind them (Freidel-Schele-Mathews 1998:90-91; Martin-Grube 2000:79). It is difficult to understand why accepted and prominent archaeologists would identify these obviously heavily pregnant females as "protector gods," and identify the manifestly apparent pyramidal temples (complete with steps leading to the top) on which the queens stand, as a litter. Published Maya art contains numerous examples of a litter, none even remotely resembling the shape of the construction shown in the graffiti drawings.

This birthing ritual in Tikal which transcended normal procedures for a routine physical birth was intended to legitimize the rule of the king and would suggest that patriarchal lineage was in name or definition only and the real power and authority to establish the lineage of kings was supplied by the queen-mother rather than the father. And these and other related religious rituals by elite females or queens were not limited to Tikal, but can be seen throughout the wide Maya territory. The vitally important role of queens and the question of whether or not there were ever any ruling queens in the patriarchal Maya polity is thoroughly analyzed and reported in Traci Arden's anthology; *Ancient Maya Women* (2002). Earlier and significant works related to the subject are those by Tatiana Proskouriakoff (1961, 1963, 1964); Joyce Marcus (1976); Linda Schele and Mary Martin (1986); and Rosemary Joyce (1992a, 1992b, 1993, 1996, 2000).

Other evidence that indicates the Queens rather than the kings controlled the dynastic lineage of Maya kings is contained in Katheryn Josserand's study of women that appear in Maya writings on important matters of state. Josserand's study presents a far different view of the so-called "patriarchal" social traditions of the Maya than that contained in current historiography. Josserand emphasizes the point that while males are usually the most prominent figures on dynastic related monuments there are a number of these monuments and works of art where an elite female is the most prominent protagonist. One such example is the Oval

Figure 12: A detail from the Palenque Oval Palace Tablet showing the queen, Lady Zak Kuk, bestowing the Crown of Rulership on her son Pacal. From Schele-Freidel (1990).

Palace Tablet in Palenque (Figure 12) which shows the young king Pacal receiving the crown and emblems of Rulership from his mother Lady Zak Kuk, identified by a name phrase around her head that begins and ends with elite female title glyphs. The queen, Lady Zak Kuk is the dominant subject of the event shown in the tablet. Josserand noted that; "Pacal is introduced *in relation* to the queen; the text identifying Pacal consists only of the phrase *her child,* Pacal, Holy King of Palenque" (Josserand 2002:115).

Figure 13: Two examples of a queen-mother in Yaxchilan conjuring an ancestor from a supernatural serpent. After Sharer (1994) and Schele-Freidel (1994).

Mathew Looper has noted that Lady Zak Kuk in the Palenque tablet is shown with her hair cut short and wearing a masculine loincloth over the traditional long dress which suggests the androgynous identity of this queen who ruled in her own right in Palenque until she anointed her son with Kingship (Looper 2002:182). And this governing tradition was not limited to Palenque and apparently was practiced throughout the Maya realm. Ruth Krochock in her study of Maya hieroglyphic inscriptions records this same Palenque religious tradition existed in Chichén Itzá where elite women and queens provided the political sanction for male succession to Rulership and elite daughters were sent to rule over tributary cities until a suitable male could be crowned king or ruler (Krochock 2002:152-170).

There is evidence that in addition to the birthing ritual and the ritual for succession to Rulership, the female queen-mother played the dominant role in other important Maya religious rituals involving creation, re-creation, or materialization of mortal ancestors and supernatural gods. An example of this role of females engaged in important religious rituals normally reserved for male hereditary high priests was carved on Lintel 25 in Yaxchilan and shown in Figure 13. This carving has been interpreted as showing Lady Xoc

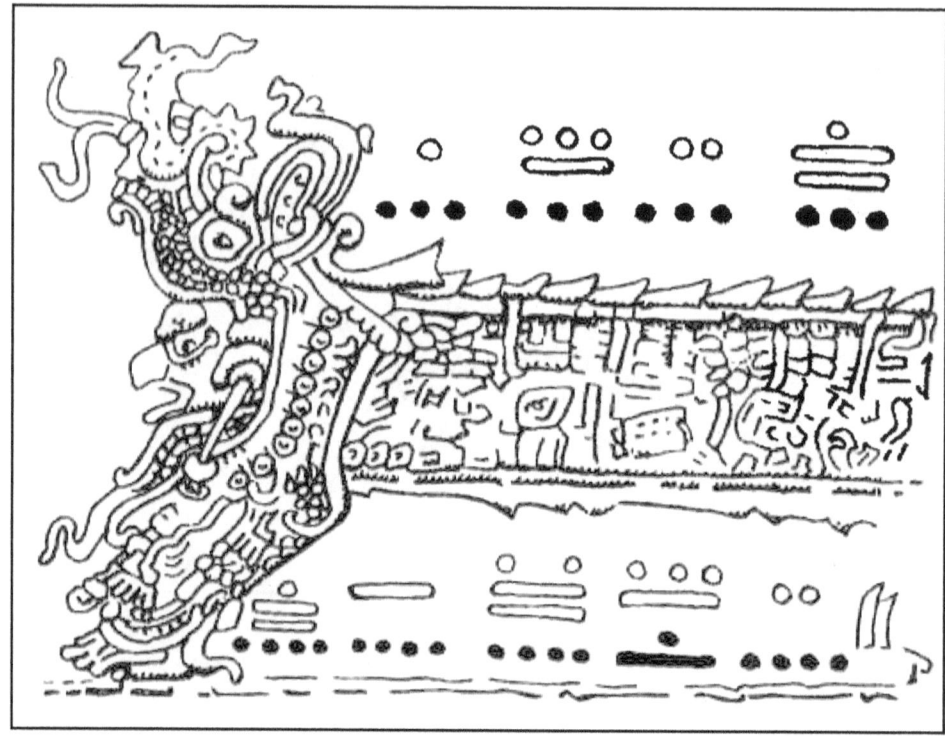

Figure 14: Drawing from the Dresden Codex of a Maya god emerging (or created) from the mouth of a supernatural earth-serpent. From Villacorta-Villacorta (1989).

the Queen-Mother performing a religious ritual involving materialization of an ancestor figure (probably Yat Balam the revered founder of Yaxchilan) from the mouth of a winged and plumed serpent (Sharer 1994:245). And a similar carving on Lintel 15 shows another Queen-Mother, Lady 6-Tun, also conjuring an ancestor from the from the mouth of a winged and plumed serpent (Schele-Freidel 1990:287), quite possibly Yat Balam's son and successor, Itzamnaaj Balam. The winged and plumed serpents in these carvings resemble the ubiquitous winged and plumed rattlesnake emblems of the Chontal/Itzá primal god Kukulcan which suggests these ancestors were from the same or related dynasty of Yax K'uk Mo, a Chontal/Itzá warlord from northern Yucatan (probably Chichén Itzá) that later in this same period (AD 426) continued south from Yaxchilan and founded Copán (Buikstra 2003; Day 2004:20-26; Peck 2005:87-90).

Analysis of these religious rituals of creation performed by Maya queen-mothers although separated in time and independent application would suggest that these religious rituals performed by the queen-mothers were based on well established and ancient religious traditions of the Olmec/Proto-Maya passed down from ancient times when female goddesses dominated their religious mystique. In this regard, the ancestor figure emerging from the mouth of a serpent in Yaxchilan is reminiscent of the Olmec god-king in Figure 5, about to emerge from the womb of the earth-mother or female Mountain of Creation with the cave opening pictured in the shape of the mouth of a serpent. The serpent has been well established as a symbol for the earth-mother and this image of a king or god being created by emerging from the mouth of a supernatural earth-serpent is also shown in the Dresden Codex (Knorozov 1982:4; Villacorta-Villacorta 1989:8). The image in the Dresden Codex (Figure 14) shows a figure with the facial features of Itzamna emerging (or being created) from the mouth of a supernatural serpent reminiscent of the pictured ritual in Figure 13. It stands to reason that the powerful Maya male priests in a strong patriarchal society would not have relinquished these important religious rituals, legitimizing (or symbolically creating) a god-king, to a female unless the ritual was deeply steeped in accepted traditions of an ancient primal First-Mother or Goddess of Creation.

Spanish colonial period documents related to Maya religious concepts of creation or origin

Spanish colonial period documents have little to say concerning the role of females in the Maya pantheon of gods or related priestly activities. The primary Spanish colonial period documents that contain limited information related to Maya religious concepts are: The Chilam Balam books, Diego de Landa's *Relación de las Cosas de Yucatan,* the Madrid and Dresden codices, and the *Popol Vuh.* Of the several Chilam Balam books only the *Book of Chilam Balam of Chumayel* and the *Book of Chilam Balam of Tizimin* are devoted to history, but in spite of some interpretations and commentary they do not contain any viable history related to early Maya religion or government. These two books are not concerned with Maya religion as a whole, but only with a small group of theocratic nobles and priests in the late Post-Classic period who were keepers of the calendrical cosmology (which had little to do with the pantheon of gods) that established the seat of the *Katun* cycle and gave legitimacy to their

Figure 15: Depiction of the goddess Chak Chel (Ix Chel) in the Madrid Codex (left) and the Dresden Codex (right). After Ardren (2002) and Villacorta-Villacorta (1989).

limited temporal role Landa supplied considerable information in his *Relación* related to customs and traditions of the Maya and revealed that Ix Chel was revered throughout the Maya area as the goddess of childbirth, medicine, and divination (Gates 1990:78,94,165; Tozzer 1941:154). Landa failed to recognize that Ix Chel was the descendent of the Maya primal "First Mother" which would have been recorded in one or more of the hundreds of books on Maya history that he ordered destroyed in a zealous overkill to establish the Christian Faith.

The Paris and Grolier codices are devoid of female figures and the Madrid and Dresden codices are almost entirely concerned with male gods associated with mundane daily life, and reflect the late Classic period patriarchal concepts in the pantheon of gods that male priests had established in religious dogma to replace the Formative period Mountain or Earth Goddess of Creation and the later unisex God of Creation (Figures

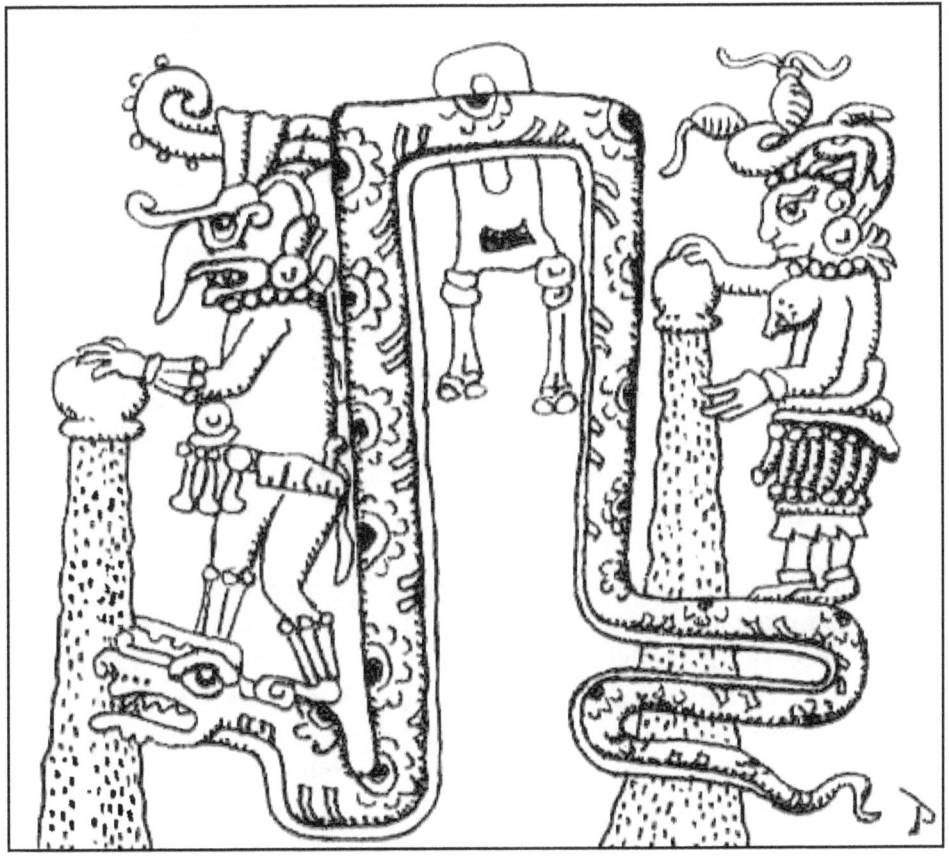

Figure 16: Drawing from the Madrid Codex showing the goddess Chak Chel and the rain god Chak pouring rain onto the earth signified by a large stylized serpent. After Ardren (2002).

7 and 8). The "First Father" and 'First Mother" survived in the names of Itzamna (First Father) and Chak Chel (First Mother). The few depictions of the goddess Chak Chel (Ix Chel) in the Madrid and Dresden codices have received various interpretations related to minor roles of this formally prominent primal Goddess of Creation. Most depictions of Chak Chel show her with a serpent headdress (Figures 14 and 15) and since the serpent has been well established since Olmec times as the emblem of Mother Earth (Figures 4, 5, and 15) the serpent headdress would tie Chak Chel to the original Olmec/Proto-Maya primal Goddess of Creation.

An illustration in the Madrid Codex also suggests Chak Chel was conceived as being associated with the ancient Goddess of Creation.

25

The drawing in the codex (Figure 15) shows Chak Chel with a writhing serpent headdress pouring life-giving rain in concert with Chak the Rain God onto the earth signified by a large stylized serpent. The serpent headdresses and other attire of Chak Chel in these late codices also contain a depiction of cotton spindles associated with the lesser roles of fertility and childbirth.

Interpretation of the true role or standing of Chak Chel in the pantheon of gods has been complicated by the widely held consensus that there were two separate female goddesses shown in the codices; the aged goddess Chak Chel (Schellhas: god O) and a young goddess Ixik Kab (Schellhas: god I) with similar features and roles to that of Chak Chel. The young goddess Ixik Kab has been interpreted as the Goddess of the Moon (Ciaramella 1994; Hofling-O'Neil 1992; Milbrath 1995, 1999:138-141, Thompson 1939, 1950:86, 1958:297-308, 1970:241-249, 1972:47-48), but the Moon Goddess aspect appears to be a bit of a stretch based on the largely irrelevant fact that in the Madrid and Dresden codices the young goddess appears in scenes related to marriage and copulation. The aged goddess Chak Chel has also been viewed as a Moon Goddess based on the questionable rationale that both goddesses are shown wearing a coiled serpent headdress (Ciaramella 1994; Milbrath 1996, 1999:143,145; Stone 1990:7,14; Taube 1992:101).

Since Chak Chel and Ixik Kab share so many of the same features including the significant coiled snake headdress (an emblem for the earth, not the moon) it would be tempting to view them as the same goddess. Traci Ardren has noted that the close association of Ixik Kab and Chak Chel with "fertility and the earth have been underemphasized in previous studies" (Ardren 2002:210) which would lend further support for the hypothesis that Chak Chel and Ixik Kab are the same late goddess of human fertility and also the early primal mother-earth Goddess of Creation which are pictured in different periods of Maya history.

The colonial period Quiché *Popol Vuh*: The "Bible" of Maya religion; or unrelated regional folklore?

The *Popol Vuh* has been labeled by Tedlock, Christenson and others as the "Maya Bible" (Christenson 2000, 2003; Tedlock 1985, 1996), but that label gives it an air of authority that it does not deserve. Dennis Tedlock in a Leap of Faith subtitled his translation and commentary as: "*The Mayan Book of the Dawn of Life*" (Tedlock (1996). The *Popol Vuh* is realistically only a book of regional folklore of the late colonial period Quiché Maya masquerading as the "Bible" of religious concepts for the large body of Formative and Classic period Maya well over a millennium earlier. In his Introduction Morley correctly identified the *Popol Vuh* as a late sacred book for only "a branch of the ancient Maya race" and suggests that the real sacred book or "Bible" was destroyed in the wholesale destruction of books in Yucatan by Landa and other clerics (Goetz-Morley 1950:ix-x). The *Popol Vuh* has endured a long and confused evolutionary history. The Preface and Introduction to the Goetz-Morley and the Tedlock edition of the *Popol Vuh* give an overview of the progression of the book from its unclear origin and translation from the Quiché language to Latin by the Dominican Priest, Francisco Ximénez, followed by several translations in Spanish, French, and German well before the English translations were published (Goetz-Morley 1950; Edmonson 1971; Tedlock 1985, 1996; Christenson 2000, 20003).

The unknown author of the *Popol Vuh,* with unclear authority and without stated foundation, attributed the Quiche Maya historical origin to the highland city of Tula. However, two instances in the narrative contradict this origin, when several of the early kings made pilgrimages and stated: "We are going to the East, *there whence came our fathers,"* and in another place they identified their origin as *"the other side of the sea"* (Goetz-Morley 1950:79-80,207, emphasis added). To the east and the other side of the sea would place their origin in the coastal areas of Yucatan rather than the highlands of Tula. Tedlock also confirmed that "the east coast of Yucatan" was the area to which the early kings of the Quiché made pilgrimages (Tedlock 1996:16). The pilgrimages to the east coast of Yucatan were ostensibly to the temples of Ix Chel, the Maya "First Mother" and fertility goddess located on Isla Mujeres and Cozumel (Gates 1990:27,165; Peck 2005a;46,179-180). It is incongruous that the Quiché kings are reported as making pilgrimages to the temples of Ix Chel, the popular and revered goddess in the "true" Maya pantheon of gods, when this well-known and documented goddess was not mentioned in the so-called "Bible," of the Quiché known as the *Popol Vuh.*

Bierhorst noted that the author of the *Popol Vuh* referred to a much earlier lost book of mythology (the true Maya Bible rather than the *Popol Vuh*) that "described how earth and sky were divided into four parts (see Figure 8) by a primal pair called Mother and Father [Ix Chel and Kukulcan/Itzamna], also known as Plumed Serpent [Kukulcan], Green Plate Spirit [earth goddess], and Blue Bowl Spirit [sky]" (Bierhorst 1990:176). Since the author of the Popol Vuh was familiar with this earlier and more authentic Maya creation mystique it is difficult to understand why this manifestly true version does not appear somewhere in his contrived version of the Maya creation mythology. Bierhorst commented on how the *Popol Vuh* presented an incomplete and distorted view of early Maya religious mythology because: "The Maya [authentic] Creation Myth is only briefly mentioned and instead, we are given the story as set forth in the first chapter of the Christian Bible, although from a distinctly Indian [Quiché Maya] point of view" (Bierhorst 1990:176).

Although the *Popol Vuh* contains no clear mention of the Maya First Mother or First Father there is a brief passage related to creation that could be referring to them by other names: "This is the account of when all is still silent and placid. All is silent and calm, hushed and empty is the womb of the sky. All alone are the Framer and the Shaper [later named Xpiyacoc and Xmucane], Sovereign and Quetzal Serpent, They Who Have Borne Children and They Who Have Begotten Sons. Luminous they are in the water, wrapped in quetzal feathers and cotinga feathers. Thus they are called Quetzal Serpent. In their essence, they are great sages, great possessors of knowledge. Thus surely there is the sky. There is also Heart of Sky, which is said to be the name of the god" (Christenson 2003:67-69).

The vital elements of this passage are unclear, ambiguous, and contradictory. It is apparent that the "Framer and Shaper" (Xpiyacoc and Xmucane) are a reference to the Maya First Mother (Ix Chel) and First Father (Itzamna) by the fact that they are referred to as "Sovereign and Quetzal Serpent," a clear reference to the primal "feathered serpent" icon seen throughout the wide Maya territory and particularly prevalent in Chichén Itzá and Yucatan. There is a clear contradiction of where this "creation" took place. One reference is creation occurred "in the water" and in another place in the "womb of the sky." Most accounts of Maya creation place it in an earthly location, either the early chaotic sea or a mountain, so the "womb of the sky" appears to be an insert by the colonial period author to accommodate the Christian belief that God resides in the heavenly sky. In like manner the nebulous god called "Heart of Sky" appears to be an arbitrary insert as he is introduced by noting that: "*There is also* Heart of Sky, *which is said to be* the name of the god (Christenson 2003:69, emphasis added). There is no role given for this almost casually mentioned god such as "Sovereign" or "Framer and Shaper," yet he appears later in several places in the *Popol Vuh* and Christenson has named him (for statistical rather than content reasons) the "principal god in the *Popol Vuh* account" (Christenson 2003:69, note 56).

After the brief introductory page, which contains some elements of early Maya creation mythology, the account of creation degenerates into a long, convoluted, frenzied, and almost grotesque version of creation that is far removed from the simple, sophisticated and intelligently understandable Maya mythology of an initial Mother-Earth Goddess of Creation followed by a First-Mother (Ix Chel), First-Father (Itzamna) and lesser gods of Rain, Maize, Fertility, and other essential elements of Maya civilization. The late Quiché regional folklore in the *Popol Vuh* pictures the "Hero Twins" as the most prominent and important gods who fought a number of supernatural demons to create, or recreate from two earlier unsuccessful attempts, mankind and the world in which we live. The myth of the Hero Twins has become so embedded in the consciousness of Maya historians that every sculpture or work of art of the Maya that contains two similar male figures, no matter how far from the Quiché in time and space, is immediately declared to represent the Hero Twins as reported in the *Popol Vuh*. The Mixtec creation mythology from contemporary colonial period sources also contained two brothers, but they do not resemble in any manner the Hero Twins of Quiché folklore since they were described as "prudent and wise in all the arts" and were the offspring of the [Maya] First Mother and First Father (Leon-Portillo and Shorris 2001:619-620).

In the Preface I emphasized the point that the omnipotent power of the Judeo/Christian and Islamic religions were responsible for suppressing the ancient Goddess of Creation religions in Europe and the Middle-East. In the Americas this suppression of the ancient Olmec/Proto-Maya Goddess of Creation religious concept has come full-circle in the *Popol Vuh* where we see the primal goddess Ix Chel mentioned (by another name) only briefly on the first page and thereafter lost from view by the prominent roles given to the male "Hero Twins" and the supreme Christianized male God known as "Heart of Sky."

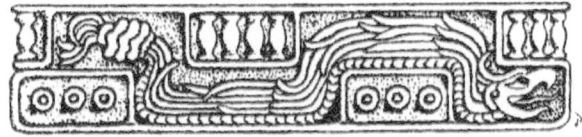

Epilogue

Contrary to what is commonly believed the large body of the Maya and other indigenous inhabitants of Mesoamerica readily accepted the dogma of Christianity to replace their established pantheon of gods. It was only the small core of priests and ruling nobles that vehemently opposed the elimination of their ancient and revered religion primarily because it was the basis for rule and control of their subjects. And when these ruling figures were removed early in the conquest, the Maya became devout Catholics with fervor that often exceeded that of their Spanish conquerors. John Lloyd Stephens traveled extensively in rural sections of Yucatan during 1841 to 1843 and reported that the vast majority of inhabitants in the rural and farming areas of Yucatan were Mayan speaking natives (still called "Indians" at that time) who seldom saw the Spanish speaking Vecinos or Mestizos in the controlling cities. These full-blooded indigenous Maya, with their own language, clung to the ancient Maya way of life, still used cacao beans for currency in their markets, and had long ago melded their ancient religious traditions including their gods and goddesses into the rituals and ceremonies of their own adopted Catholic Faith. The Maya were devout Catholics who believed that they, rather than the Spanish Vecinos, were true believers and called themselves the *Cruzob* or "People of the Cross."

Francisco Hernández de Córdoba in his 1517 discovery of Yucatan and Juan de Grijalva in his more extensive exploration of Mexican shores in 1518 carried no priests on their voyages and made no evangelical attempt to introduce the Christian Faith. Although the 1519 follow-on expedition of Hernán Cortés was essentially a military conquest; Cortés was a devout Catholic and felt that he had a paramount mission to convert the "pagans" of this new land to the Christian Faith. Cortés had a priest on every one of his ships, but these were trained and ordained only to conduct services

31

for the Spanish crew and were not capable nor did they have an interest in conversion of the inhabitants of this new land. In every case after obtaining military control of an area (in some cases after a pitched battle and in others after only a threat of military force) Cortés assembled the leading nobles and assumed his strongly ingrained role as an evangelist and proceeded to instruct his audience in Christian dogma and ordered that they must abandon their false gods and replace their idols with the Christian cross and with pictures and images of the Holy Mother Mary. In his evangelical zeal Cortés apparently spent a considerable amount of time overseeing his ship's carpenters in erecting large well-made crosses and alters from lumber hewed and fashioned from the large ubiquitous ceiba trees.

An example of Cortés' significant evangelical efforts occurred after a fierce battle with a large force of Maya warriors defending the city of Potonchan. Instead of punishing or executing the rulers of the captured city, as the Maya would have done, Cortés only lightly chided the rulers for unwisely opposing Spanish sovereignty which caused them much grief and bloodshed and then entered into what by this time had no doubt become a well rehearsed and elaborate sermon on the principal tenants of Christian religion. Cortés must have been pleasantly surprised when the native leaders seemed to readily accept his picture of Christianity as explained in his impromptu sermon. The Christian cross was accepted without opposition in their temples because they would have equated it with their stylized "Tree of Life" which was in the form of a cross. But it was the image of the Holy Mother Mary that most appealed to them. Bernal Diaz explained this welcomed reaction:

> The Caciques replied that they liked the look of the great *Teleciguata* (for in their language great ladies are called *Teleciguata*) and begged that she [the image of the Holy Mother Mary] might be given to them to keep in their town, and Cortés said that the image should be given to them, and ordered them to make a well constructed altar, and this they did at once" (Diaz del Castillo 1933:111).

Cortés and later sixteenth-century chroniclers interpreted (or misinterpreted) this desire of the Maya to display the image of the Holy Mother Mary in their temples as an immediate acceptance of the Christian Faith. It is doubtful that the Maya leaders in the audience understood the abstruse mysticism of the Holy Mother Mary and the immaculate birth of

Jesus and in saying; "they liked the look of the great *Teleciguata*" ostensibly considered this just an elegant image of their revered primal goddess Ix Chel, goddess of the related aspects of fertility and childbirth. Cortés' explanation of Mary's "immaculate birth" of the lesser god called "Jesus" would be readily accepted by the Maya because their goddess Ix Chel gave birth to the lesser Chac gods without a hint of normal copulation with a male god. Another unrelated reason why the Maya would like the look of the great *Teleciguata* was because the typical Spanish highly professional statues of the Holy Mother Mary expertly painted with realistic features and elaborately clothed would outshine their local relatively crude statues of Ix Chel.

Landa reported that the Maya from across their wide realm made long pilgrimages to the temples of the revered goddess Ix Chel on Cozumel. And there is no evidence that similar pilgrimages were made to worship the male supreme god Itzamna, or the lesser but important male gods of rain and maize. It is inconceivable that the Maya would make these long and arduous pilgrimages just to insure the fertility of their wives, so it is manifestly apparent that the driving force for the pilgrimage was an inborn recognition that Ix Chel was the embodiment of the ancient Goddess of Creation of all mankind and the earth and cosmos. And in their early conversion to Christianity this strong inborn reverence for Ix Chel did not die out, but was replaced by the current reverence amounting to worship of the Holy Mother Mary.

The writings of Don Antonio Valeriano (Poole 1997; Smith 1983:123-135) record the 1531 appearance of the Holy Mother Mary to an elderly widower named Juan Diego. Juan Diego was baptized in 1524 and described as a humble, good, and devout man and was about fifty-seven years old when the appearance of the Virgin Mary occurred. Extensive pilgrimages from across Mexico have been made to the temple erected on the site of the vision now known as the Virgin of Guadalupe and the canonization of Juan Diego was announced on 20 December, 2001. The extensive pilgrimages to the temple of the Virgin of Guadalupe suggests a strong parallel to the earlier extensive pilgrimages to the temples of Ix Chel on Cozumel.

Bibliography

Adams, Richard E. W.
  1977   *The Origins of Maya Civilization.* University of New Mexico Press, Albuquerque.
  1991   *Prehistoric Mesoamerica.* University of Oklahoma Press, Norman.

Ardren, Traci, ed.
  2002   *Ancient Maya Women.* Altamira Press, Walnut Creek, CA.

Bandelier, Adolpho F.
  1880   "On the social organization and mode of government of the ancient Mexicans," *Peabody Museum, Harvard University, 12th Annual Report,* Cambridge, Vol 2, pp. 557-699.

Barrera Vasquez, Alfredo.
  1948   *El Libro de los Libros de Chilam Balam.* Fondo de Cultura Economica, Mexico City, MX.

Bassie, Karen.
  1989   "Maya Creator Gods," in *Mesoweb,* Internet.

Bassie-Sweet, Karen.
  1991   *From the Mouth of the Dark Cave: Commemorative Sculpture of the Late Classic Maya.* University of Oklahoma Press, Norman.
  1996   *At the Edge of the World.* University of Oklahoma Press, Norman.

Baudez, Claude-Francois.
  1999   "Los templos enmascarados de Yucatan," in *Arqueologia Mexicana,* Vol. VII, #37, pp. 54-59.

Benson, Elizabeth P., ed.
- 1968   *Dumbarton Oaks Conference on the Olmec.* Dumbarton Oaks, Washington, DC.
- 1972   *The Cult of the Feline.* Dumbarton Oaks, Washington, DC.
- 1981   *The Olmec and Their Neighbors.* Dumbarton Oaks, Washington, DC.
- 1998   "The Lord, The Ruler: Jaguar Symbolism in the Americas," in N. J. Saunders ed., *Icons of Power: Feline Symbolism in the Americas,* Routledge, London, pp. 53-76.

Bernal, Ignacio.
- 1968   "View of Olmec Culture," *Dumbarton Oaks Conference on the Olmecs,"* Dumbarton Oaks Research Library and Collection, Washington, DC., pp. 135-142.
- 1969   *The Olmec World,* trans. Doris Heyden and Fernando Horcasitas, University of California Press, Berkeley.

Bierhorst, John.
- 1974   *Four Masterworks of American Indian Literature,* New York.
- 1990   *The Mythology of Mexico and Central America.* William Morrow and Company, New York.

Brasseur de Bourbourg, Charles Etienne.
- 1861   *Popol Vuh: Le Livre sacré et les mythes de l'antiquite américaine.* Collection de Documents dans les Langues Indigenes de l'Amérique Ancienne 1, Artrus Bertrand, Paris.

Buikstra, Jane E., T. D. Price, L. E. Wright, and J. A. Burton.
- 2003   "Revised Provenance of Yax K'uk Mo." Chapter 10 of *Understanding Early Classic Copán,* see, Bell 2003.

Buisseret, David, ed.
- 2006   *The Oxford Companion to Exploration.* Oxford University Press, Oxford and New York.

Cann, Rebecca L., Mark Stoneking, and Alan Wilson.
- 1987   "Mitochondrial DNA and Human Evolution," in *Nature,* Vol. 325, pp. 31-36.

Caso, Alfonso.
    1969   *The Olmec World*, trans. Doris Hyden and Fernando Horcasitas, University of California Press, Berkeley.

Caso, Alfonso, and Ignacio Bernal.
    1952   Urnas de Oaxaca, in *Memorias del Instituto Nacional de Antropologia e Historia,* Vol. 2, Biblioteca Nacional, Mexico City.

Certeau, Michael de.
    1988   *The Writing of History.* Translated by Tom Conley, Columbia University Press, New York.

Chamberlain, Robert S.
    1966   *The Conquest and Colonization of Yucatan, 1517-1550.* Reprint of the 1948 Publication #582, Carnegie Institution of Washington, by Octagon Books, Inc., New York.

Christenson, Allen J.
    2000   *Popol Vue: The Mythic Sections.* Brigham Young University Press, Salt Lake City.
    2003   *Popol Vue—The Sacred Book of the Maya.* O Books, Winchester, UK, New York.

Ciaramella, Mary.
    1994   "The Lady with the Snake Headdress," in *Seventh Palenque Roundtable,* ed. Merle Greene Robertson and Virginia M. Field, San Francisco Pre-Columbian Art Research Institute.

Coe, Michael D.
    1965a   *The Jaguar's Children: Pre-Classic Central Mexico.* The Museum of Primitive Art, New York.
    1965b   "The Olmec Style and its Distributions," in *Handbook of Middle American Indians,* Vol. 3, #2, University of Texas Press, Austin
    1967   "San Lorenzo and the Olmec Civilization," in Benson, *Dumbarton Oaks Conference on the Olmec.* Dumbarton Oaks, Washington, DC.
    1968a   *America's First Civilization.* American Heritage Publishing Company, New York.

1968b   "San Lorenzo and the Olmec Civilization," in Benson, *Dumbarton Oaks Conference on the Olmec,* Washington, DC, pp. 41-78).

1972   "Cultural Contact between the lowland Maya and Teotihuacan as seen from Tikal, Guatemala," in *Teotihuacan, XI Mesa Redonda,* Sociedad Mexicana de Antropologia, Mexico City, pp. 257-271.

1972   "Olmec Jaguars and Olmec Kings," in Benson, ed., *The Cult of the Feline* (1972:1-12).

1977   "Olmec and Maya: A Study of Relationships," in *The Origins of Maya Civilization,* ed. Richard Press, Princeton.

1989   "The Olmec Heartland: Evolution of Ideology," in *Regional Perspectives on the Olmec,* ed.

Robert J. Sharer and David C. Grove, Cambridge, pp. 68-82.

1993   *The Maya* (fifth edition). Thames and Hudson, London.

2002   *Mexico: From the Olmecs to the Aztecs.* Thames and Hudson, London.

Coe, Michael D., R. A. Diehl, and M. Stuiver.

1967   "Olmec Civilization, Veracruz, Mexico: Dating of the San Lorenzo Phase," *Science*, Vol. 155, #3768, Washington DC.

Coe, Michael D., and Richard A. Diehl.

1980a   *In the Land of the Olmec—Excavations and Human Ecology at the Olmec San Lorenzo Site.* Vol 1, University of Texas Press, Austin.

1980b   *In the Land of the Olmec—The People of the River.* Vol. 2, University of Texas Press, Austin.

Cogolludo—see Lopez de Cogolludo.

Cortés, Hernán.

1985   *Colección de Documentos Inéditos para la Historia de España,* contained in, *Cartas de Relación, Historia 16* [1852], ed., Mario Hernández, Biblioteca National, Madrid.

1889   *Hernán Cortés Copias de Documentos en el Archivo de Indias, sobre la Conquista de Mexico,* Seville, extract contained in Wagner 1942a:31.

Covarrubias, Miguel.

1929   "Notes on Mexican Masks, translated by William Spratling, *Mexican Folkways,* Vol.5, pp. 114-117.

1942   "Origen y Desarrollo del estilo artistico 'Olmeca'," in *Mayas y Olmecas: Segunda Reunión de Mesa Redonda Sobre Problemas Antropologicos de Mexico y Centro America,* Tuxtla Gutiérrez, Mexico City, pp. 46-49.

1944   "La Venta: Colossal Heads and Jaguar Gods," *Dyn,* Vol, 6, ppp. 24-33.

1946   *Mexico South, the Isthmus of Tehuantepec.* Alfred Knopf, Inc., New York.

1946a   "El Atrte 'Olmeca' o de La Venta," *Cuadernos Americanos,* Vol. XXVIII, num. 4, pp. 153-179, Mexico City, MX.

1946b   "Olmec Art or the Art of La Venta," trans. Robert T. Piazzini, in *Pre-Columbian Art History: Selected Readings,* ed. Alana Cordy-Collins and Jean Stern, University of California, Palo Alto.

1957   *Indian Art of Mexico and Central America.* Alfred Knopf, Inc., New York.

Davis, Whitney.

1978   "The So-Called Jaguar-Human Copulation Scenes in Olmec Art," *American Antiquity,* Vol. 43 #3, pp. 453-457.

Day, Charles.

2004   "Isotopic Analysis of Teeth and Bones Solves a Mesoamerican Mystery," *Physics Today,* Vol. 57, #1, pp. 20-26.

Derevianko, A. P.

1978   "On the Migrations of Ancient Man from Asia to America in the Pleistocene Epoch," pp. 70-72, Edmonton Archaeological Researches International, Dikov, Netherlands.

Diaz del Castillo, Bernal.

1933   *The Discovery and Conquest of Mexico,* an English edition of, *Historia Veradera de la Conquista de Nueva España,* as edited into modern Spanish from the original transcript in Guatemala by Genaro Garcia, translated by Alfred P. Maudslay,(second printing of 1928 edition), George Routledge & Sons, London.

Diaz, Fray Juan.

1942   *Itinerario de Larmata del re Catholico en India Uersola Isola de Iuchathan del Anno MD XVIII* (circa 1519), extract contained in

Wagner, *The Discovery of New Spain in 1518,* The Cortés Society, Berkeley.

Diehl, Richard A.
1981   "Olmec Architecture: A Comparison of San Lorenzo and La Venta," in *The Olmec and Their Neighbors: Essays in Memory of Matthew W. Stirling,* ed. Elizabeth P. Benson, Dumbarton Oaks, Washington, DC, pp. 69-82.
1989   "Olmec Architecture: What We Know and What We Wish We Knew," in *Regional Perspectives on the Olmec,* ed. Robert J. Sharer and David C. Grove, Cambridge, pp. 23-26.
2004   *The Olmecs: America's First Civilization.* Thames and Hudson, New York, London.

Diehl, Richard A., and Robert A. Benfer.
1975   "Tollan: The Toltec Capital," *Archaeology,* Vol. 28, #2, pp. 112-124.

Diehl, Richard A., and Michael D. Coe.
1995   "Olmec Archaeology," in *The Olmec World—Ritual and Rulership.* The Art Museum, Princeton University, Princeton.

Drennan, R. D.
1976   "Religion and social evolution in formative Mesoamerica," in Flannery, *The Early Mesoamerican Village,* Academic Press, New York.

Druker, Philip.
1952   "La Venta, Tabasco: A Study of Olmec Ceramics and Art," *Bureau of American Ethnology, Bulletin 153,* Smithsonian Institution, Washington, DC.
1961   "The La Venta Olmec Support Area," *Kroeber Anthropological Society Papers,* No. 35, pp. 59-72, University of California, Berkeley.
1981   "On the Nature of Olmec Polity," in *The Olmec and Their Neighbors: Essays in Memory of Matthew W. Stirling,* ed. Elizabeth P. Benson, Dumbarton Oaks, Washington, DC.

Durán, Diego.
1971   *Book of the Gods and Rites and the Ancient Calendar.* University of Oklahoma Press, Norman.

1994   *The History of the Indies of New Spain.* Translated with commentary and Introduction by Doris Heyden, University of Oklahoma Press, Norman.

Edmonson, Munro S.
1971   *The Book of Counsel: The Popol Vuh of the Quiche Maya of Guatemala.* Middle American Research Institute Publication 35, Tulane University, New Orleans.
1982   *The Ancient Future of the Itzá: The Book of Chilam Balam of Tizimin.* University of Texas Press, Austin.
1986   *Heaven Born Mérida and its Destiny—The Book of Chilam Balam of Chumayel.* University of Texas Press, Austin.
1988   *The Book of the Year: American Calendrical Systems,* University of Utah Press, Salt Lake City, Utah.

Eliade, Mircea.
1959   *The Sacred and the Profane: The Nature of Religion.* Translated from the French by Willard R. Trask, Harper and Row, New York.
1964   *Shamanism, Archaic Techniques of Ecstacy.* Routlage and Keegan Paul, Princeton.

Flannery, Kent V., and Joyce Marcus.
1976   "Evolution of the public building in Oaxaca," in Charles Cleland, ed., *Cultural Change and Continuity.* Academic Press, New York.
2000   "Formative Mexican Chiefdoms and the myth of the 'Mother Culture,' *Journal of Anthropological Archaeology,* Vol. 19, pp. 1-37.

Forsteman, Ernst Wilhelm.
1989   *Commentary on the Maya Manuscript in the Royal Public Library of Dresden,* trans. Selma Wesselhoeft and A. M. Parker, Papers of the Peabody Museum of Archaeology and Ethnology. The Peabody Museum, Cambridge, 4, #2, unabridged reprint of the 1906 edition, Aegean Park Press, Laguna Hills CA.

Freidel, David
1979   "Culture areas and interaction spheres: contrasting approaches to the emergence of civilization in the Maya lowlands," *American Antiquity,* Vol. 44, pp. 36-54.

1981   "Civilization as a state of mind; the cultural evolution of the
        Lowland Maya," in Jones-Kautz, *The Transition to Statehood in
        the New World* (1981:188-227).

Freidel, David, Linda Schele, and Joy Parker.
1993   *Maya Cosmos: Three Thousand Years on the Shamans Path.* William
        Morrow and Company, New York.

Friedman J., and M. J. Rowlsnds, eds.
1978   *Evolution of Social Systems.* Duckworth, Ltd., London.

Fuente, Beatriz de la.
1977   *Los Hombres de Piedra: Escultura Olmeca,* Biblioteca Cultura,
        Mexico City.
1981   Toward a Conception of Olmec Monumental Art, in *The Olmec
        and Their Neighbors: Essays in Memory of Matthew W. Stirling,*
        ed. Elizabeth P. Benson, Dumbarton Oaks, Washington, DC.
1992   "Order and Nature in Olmec Art," in *The Ancient Americas: Art
        from Sacred Landscapes,* ed. Richard F. Townsend, Chicago, 121-
        133.

Furst, Peter T.
1968   "The Olmec Were-Jaguar Motif in the Light of Ethnographic
        Reality," in *Dumbarton Oaks Conference on the Olmec,* Washington
        DC., pp. 143-174.
1981   "Jaguar Baby or Toad Mother: A New Look at an Old Problem in
        Olmec Iconography," in *The Olmec and Their Neighbors,* edited
        by E. P. Benson, Dumbarton Oaks, Washington DC.

Gadon, Elinor W.
1989   *The Once and Future Goddess: A Sweeping Visual Chronicle
        of the Sacred Female.* Harper and Row, Publishers, New York,
        London.

Garcia de Palacio, Diego.
1866   *Relación hecho por el Licenciado Palacio al Rey D. Felipe II
        en la que describe la provincia de Guatemala."* In *Colección de
        documentos inéditos de Indias* Vol. VI, Madrid.

Gates, William.
    1990   *Yucatan Before and After the Conquest,* translation with up-dated commentary of Diego de Landa's *Relación de las Cosas de Yucatan.* Producion Editorial Dante, Merida, MX.

Gay, Carlo T. E.
    1972   *Chalcatcingo.* International Scholarly Book Services, Portland.

Gimbutas, Marija.
    1999   *The Living Goddesses.* University of California Press, Berkeley.

Goetz, Delia, and Sylvanus Morley.
    1950   *Popol Vuh.* University of Oklahoma Press, Norman.

Gómez, Emilio Abreu.
    1979   *Canek—History and Legend of a Maya Hero.* Translated with introduction by Mario L. Davila and Carter Wilson, University of California Press, Berkeley and London.

Grove, David C.
    1974   "The Highland Olmec Manifestation: A consideration of what is and what isn't," *Mesoamerican Archaeology: New Approaches,* University of Texas Press, Austin.
    1976   "Olmec Origins and Transpacific Diffusion: Reply to Meggers," *American Anthropologist,* Vol. 78, #4, pp. 634-637.
    1984   *Chalcatzingo—Excavations on the Olmec Frontier,* Thames and Hudson Ltd., London.
    1989   "Olmec: What's in a Name?" In *Regional Perspectives on the Olmec,* edited by R. J. Sharer and D. C. Grove, Cambridge University Press, Cambridge, pp. 8-14.

Grove David C., Kenneth Hirth, David Buge, and Ann Cyphers.
    1976   "Formative period settlement and cultural development at Chalcatzingo, Morelos, Mexico," *Science,* Vol. 192, pp. 12031210.

Guthrie, Jill, ed.
    1995   *The Olmec World—Ritual and Rulership.* The Art Museum, Princeton University, Princeton.

Hofling, Charles A., and Thomas O'Neil.
1992 "Eclipse Cycles in the Moon Goddess Almanacs in the Dresden Codex," in *The Sky in Mayan Literature,* ed. Anthony F. Aveni, pp. 102-132, Oxford University Press, New York.

Joralemon, P. David.
1971 "A Study of Olmec Iconography," in *Studies in Pre-Columbian Art and Archaeology, #7,* Dumbarton Oaks, Washington, DC.
1976 "The Olmec Dragon: A Study in Pre-Columbian Iconography," in *Origins of Religious Art and Iconography in Preclassic Mesoamerica, ed. Henry B. Nicholson,* (1976:27-71).

Joyce, Rosemary A.
1992 "Images of Gender and Labor Organization in Classic Maya Society," in *Exploring Gender through Archaeology: Selected Papers from the 1991 Boone Conference*, ed. Cheryl Claassen, Prehistory Press, Madison.
1993 "Women's Work: Images of Production and Reproduction in Pre-Hispanic Southern Central America," *Current Anthropology,* Vol. 34, pp. 255-274.
2000 *Gender and Power in Prehispanic Mesoamerica.* University of Texas Press, Austin.

Joyce, Rosemary A., and Cheryl Claassen.
1997 "Women in the Ancient Americas: Archaeologists, Gender, and the Making of Prehistory," in *Women in Prehistory: North America and Mesoamerica,* ed. Cheryl Claassen and Rosemary A. Joyce, University of Pennsylvania Press, Philadelphia.

Knorozov, Yuri V.
1982 *Maya Hieroglyphic Codices.* Translated by Sophie Coe, Institute for Mesoamerican Studies, State University of New York, Albany.

Landa, Diego de.
1941 *Relación de las Cosas de Yucatan* [1566]. Translated into modern Spanish, Producción Editorial Dante, Merida, Yucatan, MX.

1941   *Landa's Relación de las Cosas de Yucatan* [1566], translated with notes by Alfred M. Tozzer, Peabody Museum of American Archaeology and Ethnology, Harvard, Cambridge, MA.

1978   *Yucatan Before and After the Conquest, by Friar Diego de Landa,* translation of Landa's *Relación de las Cosas de Yucatan,* with notes by William Gates. Reprint of Publication #20, The Maya Society, Baltimore (1937), Dover Publications, Inc., New York.

1990   *Yucatan Before and After the Conquest, by Friar Diego de Landa,* translation of Landa's *Relación de las Cosas de Yucatan* [1566], by William Gates with commentary and appendix, Producción Editorial Dante, Merida, MX.

Laymon, Charles M., ed.
1971   *The Interpreters One Volume Commentary on the Bible.* Abingdon Press, Nashville and New York

Leeming, David, and Margaret Leeming.
1994   *A Dictionary of Creation Myths.* Oxford University Press, Inc., New York.

Leeming, David, ed.
2005   *The Oxford Companion to World Mythology.* Oxford University Press, Inc., New York.

León-Portilla, Miguel.
1963   *Aztec Thought and Culture: A Study of the Ancient Nahuatl Mind.* University of Oakhoma Press, Norman.

1968a   *Quetzalcoatl.* Fondo de Cultura Economica, Mexico City.

1968b   *Trempo e Realidad en el Pensa miento Maya.* Nacional Biblioteca, Mexico City.

1969   *Pre-Columbian Literature of Mexico.* University of Oklahoma Press, Norman.

1973   *Time and Reality in the Thought of the Maya.* Universidad Nacional Autónoma de México Ciudad Universitaria (1968). English edition by Beacon Press, Boston.

1992   *Literasturas Indigenas de Mexico,* Fondo de Cultura Economica, Mexico City. English extract translation contained in (León-Portilla,-Shorris 2001).

León-Portilla, Miguel, and Earl Shorris.
2001   *In the Language of Kings: An Anthology of Mesoamerican Literature-Pre-Columbian to the Present,* W. W. Norton & Company, New York and London.

Levy, Janet E.
1999   "Gender, Power, and Heterarchy in Middle-Level Societies," in Sweeny (1999:62-78).

Levy, Rachel.
1948   *The Gate of Horn; A Study of the Religious Conceptions of the Stone Age, and Their Influence on European Thought.* Faber & Faber, Ltd., London.

López de Cogolludo, Diego.
1867   *Historia de Yucatan* (2 Vols.). Translation of the original 1688 document into modern Spanish, Producción Editorial Dante, Biblioteca Cultura, Merida.
!957   *Historia de Yucatan* [2 Vols.]. Colección de Grande Cronicas Mexicanos, Editorial Academia Liberaria; first published in 1688, fifth edition translated into modern Spanish, Mexico City, MX.

Lowie, R. H.
1963   *Indians of the Plains.* Natural History Press, Garden City.

Luckert, Karl W.
1976   *Olmec Religion: A Key to Middle America and Beyond.* University of Oklahoma Press, Norman.

Marcus, Joyce.
1992   *Mesoamerican Writing Systems: Propaganda, Myths, and History in Four Ancient Civilizations,* Princeton University Press, Princeton.
1993   "Ancient Maya Political Organization," in *Lowland Maya Civilization in the Eighth Century AD.* Dumbarton Oaks, Washington, DC.
2003   "The Maya and Teotihuacan," in Braswell, ed., *The Maya and Teotihuacan: Reinterpreting Early Classic Interaction,* (2003:337-356).

Markman, Peter T., and Roberta H. Markman.
1989   *Masks of the Spirit: Image and Metaphor in Mesoamerica.* University of California Press, Berkeley.

Martinez Hernández, Juan.
1926   *Crónica de Yaxkukul,* Documentos Cultura, Merida.

Martin, Simon, and Nikolai Grube.
2000   *Chronicle of the Maya Kings and Queens.* Thames and Hudson, London.

Milbrath, Susan.
1995   "Gender and Roles of Lunar Dieties in Postclassic Central Mexico and Their Correlations with the Maya Area," in *Estudios de Cultura Nahuatl,* Vol 25, pp. 45-93.
1979   *A Study of Olmec Sculptural Chronology.* Studies in Pre-Columbian Art and Archaeology, #23, Dumbarton Oaks, Washington, DC.
1999   *Star Gods of the Maya—Astronomy in Art, Folklore, and Calendars.* University of Texas Press, Austin.

Miller, Mary E., and Karl Taube.
1993   *The Gods and Symbols of Ancient Mexico and the Maya: An Illustrated Dictionary of Mesoamerican Religion.* Thames and Hudson, London.

Morley Sylvanus G.
1956   *The Ancient Maya.* Stanford University Press, Stanford.

Murdy, Carson N.
1981   "Congenital Deformaties and the Olmec Were-Jaguar Motif," *American Antiquity,* Vol. 46, #4, pp. 861-871.

Patai, Raphael.
1967   *The Hebrew Goddess.* Avon Books, New York.

Peck, Douglas T.
1998   "Anatomy of an Historical Fantasy: The Ponce de León-Fountain of Youth Legend," *Revista de Historia de America,* Numero 123,

Instituto Panamericano de Geografia e Historia, Mexico City, MX.

2002　"The Geographical Origin and Acculturation of Maya Advanced Civilization in Mesoamerica," *Revista de Historia de America,* Instituto Panamericano de Geografia e Historia, Numero 130, Mexico City, Mx.

2005a　*The Yucatan—From Prehistoric Times to the Great Maya Revolt of 1546.* Xlibris Corporation, Philadelphia.

2005b　"Reexamination of Spanish Colonial Period Documents Related to Prehistoric Maya History and Mythology," *Revista de Historia de America,* Numero 136, Mexico City, pp. 21-35.

2006　"Mythical Lands in Early Cartography," *The Portolan,* Fall, #66.

2007a　*Origin and Diffusion of Maya Civilization.* Xlibris Corporation, Philadelphia.

2007c　"Ponce de León, Juan (1474-1521)," in *The Oxford Companion to World Exploration* (2 vols.), Oxford University Press, Oxford & New York, pp. (2):170-171.

Pohorilenko, Anotole.

1977　"On the Question of Olmec Deities," *Journal of New World Archaeology,* Vol. 2, pp. 1-16.

Pool, Christopher A.

2007　*Olmec Archaeology and Early Mesoamerica.* Cambridge University Press, Cambridge.

Poole, Stafford.

1997　*Our Lady of Guadalupe: The Origins and Sources of a Mexican National Symbol.* University of Arizona Press, Tucson.

Proskouriakoff, Tatiana.

1951　"Some non-Classic traits in the sculpture of Yucatan," in *The Civilization of Ancient America,* selected papers of the 29th International Congress of Americanists, ed. Sol Tax, Chicago. pp. 108-118.

1961　"Portraits of Women in Maya Art," in *Essays in Pre-Columbian Art and Archaeology,* ed. Samuel K. Lothrop et al., pp. 81-99, Harvard University Press, Cambridge.

1963　"Historical Data in the Inscriptions of Yaxchilan, Part I, *Estudios de Cultura Maya,* Vol. 3.

1964   "Historical Data in the Inscriptions of Yaxchilan, Part II, *Estudios de Cultura Maya,* Vol. 4.

1968   "Olmec and Maya Art: Problems of Their Stylistic Relation," in Benson *Dumbarton Oaks Conference on the Olmec,* Dumbarton Oaks, Washington, DC.

1987   *Monograph and Papers in Maya Archaeology.* Peabody Museum of Archaeology and Ethnology, Vol. 67, Harvard, pp. 459-467.

Recinos, Adrian.
1953   *Popol Vuh: Las Antiguas Historias del Quiché.* Fondo de Cultura Económica, Mexico City.

Roys, Ralph L.
1943   *The Indian Background of Colonial Yucatan.* Publication 548, Carnegie Institution of Washington, Washington, DC.

1952   *Conquest Sites and the Subsequent Destruction of Maya Architecture in the Interior of Northern Yucatan.* Carnegie Institution of Washington, Publication #596.

1967   *The Book of Chilam Balam of Chumayel.* Reprint of Carnegie Institution of Washington, Publication #538 (1933), Washington DC, University of Oklahoma Press, Norman.

Sahagún, Bernardino de.
1932   *A History of Ancient Mexico by Fray Bernardino de Sahagún.* Translated by Fannie R. Bandelier, Fiske University Press, Nashville.

1963   *The Florentine Codex: Earthly Things*, translated by Arthur Anderson and Charles Dibble, The School of American Research and University of Utah, Santa Fe, NM.

Schele, Linda.
1995   "The Olmec Mountain and Tree of Creation in Mesoamerican Cosmology," in, *The Olmec World: Ritual and Rulership,* The Art Museum, Princeton University, Princeton.

Schele, Linda, and Mary Ellen Miller.
1986   *The Blood of Kings: Dynasty and Ritual in Maya Art.* Kimbal Art Museum, Fort Worth.

Schele, Linda, and David Freidel.
1990   *A Forest of Kings—The Untold Story of the Ancient Maya.* William Morrow, New York.

Schele, Linda, and Peter Mathews.
1998   *The Code of Kings.* Simon and Schuster, New York.

Schellhas, Paul.
1904   "Representation of Deities of the Maya Manuscripts," *Papers of the Peabody Museum of American Archaeology and Ethnology,* Vol. 4, #1, Harvard University, Cambridge.

Scholes, France V., and Ralph L. Roys.
1968   *The Maya Chontal Indians of Acalan-Tixchel,* Reprint of Carnegie Institution 1948 edition with commentary, University of Oklahoma Press, Norman.

Sharer, Robert J.
1983   "Interdisciplinary Approaches to the Study of Mesoamerican Highland-Lowland Interaction: A Summary View," in *Highland-Lowland Interaction in Mesoamerica: Interdisciplinary Approaches,* Dumbarton Oaks, Washington DC. (1983:241-263).
1994   *The Ancient Maya.* Fifth edition, Stanford University Press, Stanford.
1997   "Kinich Yax K'uk" Mo' and the Genesis of the Copan Acropolis," paper presented at the symposium *A Tale of Two Cities: Copan and Teotihuacan,* Harvard University.
1999   "Tikal and the Copan Dynastic Founding," School of American Research Advanced Seminar, "Changing Perspectives on Tikal and the Development of Ancient Maya Civilization," Sante Fe. NM.

Sharp, Rosemary.
1981   "Chacs and Chiefs: The Iconology of Mosaic Sculpture in Pre-Conquest Yucatan," *Studies in Pre-Columbian Art & Archaeology,* #24, Dumbarton Oaks, Washington DC.

Sjoo, Monica & Barbara Mor.
1987   *The Great Cosmic Mother: Rediscovering the Religion of the Earth.* Harper-Collins Publishers, San Francisco.

Smith, Jody Brant.
    1983   *The Image of Guadalupe.* Doubleday & Company, Inc., New York.

Soustelle, Jacques.
    1985   *The Olmecs: The Oldest Civilization in Mexico.* Translated by Helen R. Lane, University of Oklahoma Press, Norman.

Spinden, Herbert J.
    1922   "Ancient Civilizations of Mexico and Central America," *Handbook Series,* Vol. 3, American Museum of Natural History, New York.
    1937   "Huastec sculpture and the Cult of Apotheosis," *The Brooklyn Museum Quarterly,* Vol. 24, #4, Brooklyn.
    1975   *A Study of Maya Art: Its Subject Matter and Development.* Unabridged republication of the 1913 edition published by the Peabody Museum of American Archaeology and Ethnology, Cambridge. Dover Publications, Inc., New York.

Stephens, John L.
    1962   *Incidents of Travel in Yucatan.* (Vol. 2) Edited with introduction by Victor Wolfgang von Hagen, University of Oklahoma Press, Norman
    1963   *Incidents of Travel in Yucatan.* (2 Vols.) Unabridged republication of the 1843 edition containing engravings and sketches by Frederick Catherwood in text and in Appendix fold-out. Dover Publications, Inc., New York.
    1969   *Incidents of Travel in Central America, Chiapas, and Yucatan.* Unabridged republication of the 1841 edition containing engravings by Frederick Catherwood. Dover Publications, Inc., New York.

Stirling, Matthew W.
    1939   "Discovering the New World's Oldest Dated Work of Man," *National Geographic Magazine,* Vol. LXXVI, pp. 183-218.
    1940a   "An Initial Series from Tres Zapotes, Vera Cruz, MX," *National Geographic Society Contributed Technical Papers,* #1, Washington DC.
    1940b   Great Stone Faces of the Mexican Jungle," *National Geographic Magazine,* Vol 78, #1.
    1943a   "La Venta's Greenstone Tigers," *National Geographic Magazine,* Vol. 84, #3.

1943b "Stone Monuments of Southern Mexico," *Bureau of American Ethnology, Bulletin 138,* Smithsonian Institution, Washington, DC.

1947 "On the Trail of the La Venta Man," *National Geographic,* Vol. KCI, #2, pp. 137-172.

1955 "Stone Monuments of the Rio Chiquito, Veracruz, Mexico," *Anthropological Papers No. 43, Bureau of American Ethnology, Bulletin 157,* pp. 1-23.

1965 "Monumental Sculpture of Southern Vera Cruz and Tabasco, in *Handbook of Middle American Indians: Archaeology of Southern Mesoamerica,* edited by Gordon R. Willey, University of Texas Press, Austin, Vol. 3 pp. 716-738.

1967 "Early History of the Olmec Problem," in *Dumbarton Oaks Conference on the Olmec,* edited by Elisabeth P. Benson, Washington, DC., 1-8

Stone, Merlin.
1976 *When God Was a Woman.* Dial Press, New York.

Sweely, Tracy L., ed.
1999 *Manifesting Power: Gender and the Interpretation of Power in Archaeology.* Routledge, London.

Tate, Carolyn E.
1987 "The Royal Women of Yaxchilán," in *Memorias del Primer Coloquie Internacional de Mayistas,* Universidad Nacional Autónoma de Mexico, Mexico City.

1992 *Yaxchilan: The Design of a Maya Ceremonial City.* University of Texas Press, Austin.

1996 "Art in Olmec Culture," in Guthrie; *The Olmec World: Ritual and Rulership* (1996).

1999a "Patrons of Shamanic Power: La Venta's Supernatural Entities in Light of Mixe Beliefs," *Ancient Mesoamerica,* Vol. 10, pp. 169-188.

1999b "Writing on the Face of the Moon: Women's Products, Archetypes, and Power in Ancient Maya Civilization," in *Manifesting Power: Gender and the Interpretation of Power in Archaeology,* ed. Tracy L. Sweely, pp. 81-102, Routledge, London.

Taube, Karl A.
    1992a   *The Major Gods of Ancient Yucatan.* Dumbarton Oaks Research Library and Collection, Washington, DC.

    1992b   "The Temple of Quetzalcoatl and the Cult of Sacred Warfare at Teotihuacan," *Anthropology and Aesthetics,* Vol. 21, pp. 53-87.

    1995   "The Rainmakers: The Olmec and Their Contribution to Mesoamerican Belief and Ritual," contained in, Guthrie, *The Olmec World—Ritual and Leadership.*

    2002   *Heaven and Hell: Portals, Xibalba, and the Flowery Paradise.* Institute of Archaeology and European Association of Mayanists—The British Museum, London.

    2003a   "Tetitla and the Maya Presence at Teotihuacan," in *The Maya and Teotihuacan: Reinterpreting Early Classic Interaction,* ed. G. E. Braswell, University of Texas Press, Austin, pp. 273-314.

    2003b   *Aztec and Maya Myths.* University of Texas Press, Austin.

    2004   "The Origin and Development of Olmec Research," in *Olmec Art at Dumbarton Oaks,* Dumbarton Oaks, Washington, DC.

Tedlock, Barbara.
    2005   *The Woman in the Shaman's Body.* Bantam Books, New York.

Tedlock. Dennis.
    1985   *Popol Vuh—The Mayan Book of the Dawn of Life.* Simon and Schuster, New York.

    1996   *Popol Vuh—The Mayan Book of the Dawn of Life.* Revised edition of the 1985 publication Simon and Schuster, New York.

Thompson, J. Eric S.
    1939   *The Moon Goddess in Middle America with Notes on Related Dieties,* Contributions to American Anthropology and History, Carnegie Institution of Washington, Publication 5, #29, Carnegie Institution, Washington, DC.

    1950   *Maya Hieroglyphic Writing: An Introduction,* Carnegie Institution of Washington Publication 589, Carnegie Institution, Washington, DC.

    1970   *Maya History and Religion.* University of Oklahoma Press, Norman.

    1972   *A Commentary on the Dresden Codex: A Maya Hieroglyphic Book,* American Philosophical Society, Philadelphia.

Tozzer, Alfred M.
  1907   *A Comparative Study of the Maya and the Lacandones.* Archaeological Institute of America, New York.
  1918   "The Domain of the Aztecs and Their Relation to the Prehistoric Cultures of Mexico," *Holmes Anniversary Volume,* Lancaster, pp. 464-468.
  1941   *Landa's Relación de las Cosas de Yucatan.* Peabody Museum of American Archaeology and Ethnology, Cambridge.
  1957   *Chichén Itzá and Its Cenote of Sacrifice.* Memoirs of the Peabody Museum of Archaeology and Ethnology, Cambridge.

Tuchman, Barbara.
  1978   *A Distant Mirror: The Calamitous 14ᵗʰ Century.* Alfred A. Knopf, New York.
  1984   *The March of Folly: From Troy to Vietnam.* Ballantine Books, New York.

Vail, Gabrielle and Andrea Stone.
  2002   "Representations of Women in Postclassic and Colonial Maya Literature and art," in Ardren, *Ancient Maya Women* (2002)

Villacorta, Carlos A. and J. Antonio Villacorta.
  1977   *Codices Maya.* Second edition reprint of the 1930 edition, Tipografia National, Guatemala.
  1989   *The Dresden Codex.* Reprint of the Dresden Codex portion of the 1930 edition of *Codices Maya.* Aegean Park Press, Laguna Hills, CA.

Xu, H. Mike.
  1996   *Origin of the Olmec Civilization.* University of Central Oklahoma Press, Edmund.

Yusuf Ali, Abdullah.
  2001   *The Holy Qur'an.* Text, Translation, and Commentary by Abdullah Yusuf Ali, Tahrike Tarsile Qur'an, Inc., Elmhurst, NY.

Index